LEADER BY ACCIDENT

Praise for
LEADER BY ACCIDENT

"The adage that good things come in small packages is proven yet again by Jim Rafferty's book *Leader by Accident*. It is a terrific book about how to be a leader but what makes it so special is that it is also about how to live a life with meaning for oneself and for others. The lessons derive from Rafferty's leadership of a Boy Scout troop after a shooting tragedy and the most poignant are expressed through his talks with the teen-age boys in the Scout troop. It is a very rare book that packs so much wisdom (and wit) about leadership and life into so few pages. I couldn't put it down."

—**Robert M. Gates**, U.S. Secretary of Defense 2006-2011,
National President of the Boy Scouts of America 2014-2016.

"The unimaginable tragedy that upturned our community inspired Jim Rafferty's journey through the perils and rewards of leadership. *Leader by Accident* is a conversation offering invaluable lessons of character, perseverance, and hope. It leaves one transformed and inspired. Timely and timeless, it's a necessary read."

—**Congressman C. A. Dutch Ruppersberger**, United States
House of Representatives, Maryland, 2nd District and Life Scout

"When an unbelievable tragedy occurred, Jim stepped outside of his comfort zone and discovered leadership qualities he never knew he had. Jim's book will make you realize we all can be leaders by accident. His personal journey is very relatable, with inspiring anecdotes that helped shape his life. His candid thoughts will make you think about taking that first step and having no regrets. Six words changed Jim's life: 'you're one of their favorite leaders.'"

—**Neil Hartman**, Award-winning television sportscaster and
current Director for the Center for Sports Communication
and Social Impact at Rowan University

"As I live in the area where Jim Rafferty's book takes place and vividly remember the tragic event that created Jim's 'accidental' fall into leadership, I read his book with great interest. I was not disappointed.

Jim, with his humor and adept storytelling, has done us all a great service. He has given us a refreshing look at how we can all stand up and be leaders. The message is pretty direct: When the call comes, and you see the opportunity, you can lead. But Jim makes no bones, leadership is not easy, he makes it clear that there are lessons everywhere and you need to be keenly aware in order to take advantage.

All in all, this is a great read that will tug at your heart, make you laugh, and provide you some great leadership wisdom."

—**Neal Woodson**, Author, *The Uncomplicated Coach*

LEADER
BY
ACCIDENT

Lessons in Leadership, Loss and Life

JIM RAFFERTY

NEW YORK

LONDON • NASHVILLE • MELBOURNE • VANCOUVER

LEADER BY ACCIDENT
Lessons in Leadership, Loss and Life

Published in New York, New York, by Morgan James Publishing. Morgan James is a trademark of Morgan James, LLC. www.MorganJamesPublishing.com

Morgan James BOGO™

A **FREE** ebook edition is available for you or a friend with the purchase of this print book.

CLEARLY SIGN YOUR NAME ABOVE

Instructions to claim your free ebook edition:
1. Visit MorganJamesBOGO.com
2. Sign your name CLEARLY in the space above
3. Complete the form and submit a photo of this entire page
4. You or your friend can download the ebook to your preferred device

ISBN 978-1-63195-465-8 paperback
ISBN 978-1-63195-466-5 eBook
Library of Congress Control Number: 2021902064

Cover Design by:
Chris Treccani
www.3dogdesign.net

Morgan James is a proud partner of Habitat for Humanity Peninsula and Greater Williamsburg. Partners in building since 2006.

Get involved today! Visit
MorganJamesPublishing.com/giving-back

To the amazing and resilient young men of Boy Scout Troop 328 of Timonium, Maryland, and to the adult leaders who gave so much.

To Monica, Matt and Megan, who encouraged and supported my steps into the unknown.

And especially to John, Tammy, Greg and Ben. Your spirit lives on in our community and in our hearts.

TABLE OF CONTENTS

Foreword   xv

Introduction   xvii

About the BSA   xix

The Scoutmaster Minute   xxii

Scoutmaster Minute: How Will You Feel if You Don't?   1

The First Days   3

Scoutmaster Minute: When Are You a Scout?   7

The First Week   9

Scoutmaster Minute: A Scout Is Brave   14

Comfort Zone   16

Scoutmaster Minute: That First Step   23

So What?   25

Scoutmaster Minute: Don't Say No   31

Your Comfort Zone   33

Scoutmaster Minute: Get Outside   39

Solitude   40

Scoutmaster Minute: Enjoy the Journey   44

Your Comfort Zone II   46

Scoutmaster Minute: The Soloist and the Group   *49*

    The Soloist, the Conductor and the Team   51

Scoutmaster Minute: We Are What We Repeatedly Do   *55*

    Learning to Lead   57

Scoutmaster Minute: The Power of the Apology   *60*

    Leadership Means Having to Say You're Sorry   62

Scoutmaster Minute: Team Effort   *66*

    Don't Go It Alone   68

Scoutmaster Minute: Thanksgiving   *73*

    Gratitude   75

Scoutmaster Minute: The Wind at Your Back   *78*

    Hold Their Attention   80

Scoutmaster Minute: Recalculating   *86*

    The Roads Not Taken   88

Scoutmaster Minute: Getting Up Again   *92*

Scoutmaster Minute: Opportunity Disguised as Failure   *94*

    Job I Was Better Than   96

Scoutmaster Minute: Teaching   *100*

    Handing Off the Ball   102

Scoutmaster Minute: The Uniform   *106*

    Father and Son   108

Scoutmaster Minute: Leader or Follower?   *112*

    The Age of the Home Run   114

Scoutmaster Minute: Inspiration on the Trail   *118*

    A Few Words   120

Scoutmaster Minute: After You   *126*

    I'm Sorry that Happened   128

Scoutmaster Minute: Not Following the Crowd   *134*

    The Paradox   136

Scoutmaster Minute: Integrity   *141*

Scoutmaster Minute: Integrity, Part II   *143*

   Integrity   144

Scoutmaster Minute: Three Guidelines   *147*

   Heads Up   149

Scoutmaster Minute: Personal Finance   *154*

Scoutmaster Minute: The Teenage Brain   *156*

   The Whole Person   159

Not a Scoutmaster Minute: Best Damn Day of My Life   *162*

   Connecting   167

Scoutmaster Minute: What Else Are We Missing?   *173*

The Final Scoutmaster Minute   *175*

   Afterword   180

   Acknowledgments   182

   About the Author   185

You who choose to lead must follow
But if you fall you fall alone
If you should stand then who's to guide you?
If I knew the way I would take you home
"Ripple" — Jerry Garcia & Robert Hunter

FOREWORD

Much has been written about well-known leaders dealing with crises, and I've read my share. Lincoln and Churchill, for example, sought their respective positions and successfully dealt with the big issues of their day. Less often do we read about a "regular" person who didn't seek the job, felt unprepared, and yet also rose to the challenge, bringing change and growth… and leadership. This is such a book, written by an "accidental" leader who stepped into a tough situation and brought his wisdom and humor to a Boy Scout troop in crisis.

The management/leadership theorist, Dr. Elliot Jacques, lists a number of key attributes an effective leader must have, including the right temperament, skills in the field of work, and an intellectual capability to handle the complexity of the job. However, one of the more interesting attributes on Dr. Jacques' list is "values," by which he meant whether the leader "values" the work an organization does.

In this book it is clear that a critical piece of Jim's success as a Scout leader was how much he valued the role the Boy Scouts can play in developing young boys, and how much he valued the boys themselves. He led both by example and by his thoughtful approach to the development process. The skills piece, as Jim will discuss, was less fully developed, but the support of other parents, and the way he used their skills to full advantage, made him an effective Scoutmaster. The ability to tie a sheepshank knot would (maybe) come later…

Many books have been written on leadership, yet there remains a shortage of leaders in all aspects of life. This book highlights ways everyone can take a leadership role and ways to make that role effective. As a retired Army officer, and retired CEO, I can attest to the value of the ideas offered in this book, and the inspirational messages that go with them.

Fred Strader
United States Army, Retired
Meredith, NH

INTRODUCTION

It was just another winter Sunday morning, until it wasn't. On February 3rd, 2008, I was the first one awake in our house, as usual. I grabbed the newspaper from the driveway, poured a coffee and settled in our sunroom, our preferred weekend morning place.

The front page of *The Baltimore Sun* had a very brief, last-minute-before-press article about four members of a family being found dead in their home in Cockeysville, Maryland, the next town north of ours. "Good Lord," I thought. "Carbon monoxide poisoning?" Cockeysville is a large and populous ZIP code, so even when I recognized the street name I didn't really expect that the story would have any personal impact.

Until I reached the final line and ice ran down my spine.

Property records indicated that the home belonged to a local attorney and his family, the article said. The Scoutmaster of our son's Boy Scout troop, John Browning, was an attorney, and I knew he and his family lived on the street in question. All three boys were members of the troop as well.

For the moment, there was nothing else; no cause of death, no names, nothing, but by the time we dropped our kids off at Sunday school an hour later, word was out: The Brownings were gone. John, his wife, Tammy, and two of their three boys were dead, and although the rumor mill was running wild, no one we encountered knew how or why.

The internet news cycle in 2008 was not what it is today, and especially with a (for the moment) local story on a Sunday, so details were a while in coming. By that afternoon, though, the awful story was complete: John, Tammy, Greg and Ben had all been shot to death, and standing accused was their oldest son, Nick, who was then 15.

The horrific details of that crime have been well documented elsewhere, and won't be revisited here, except to say that it would rock our little part of the world in a seismic fashion.

A Scout troop is comprised of young people (all young men at the time) between the ages of 11 and 17, and Troop 328 numbered about 25 scouts at the time. Suddenly that number was reduced by three, and every single scout had lost at least one friend, if not two or three, in addition to their beloved Scoutmaster. More than a decade later, it's still almost unimaginable to me.

How would the troop survive something like this? Would the troop survive at all? Finding the answers to those questions would prove to be life-changing for me in ways I could not have imagined at the time.

ABOUT THE BSA

In many ways, the Boy Scouts of America (the BSA in my day, but now known as "Scouts USA" since girls are welcome as well) is an anachronism. Sit around a campfire, perform hokey skits and sing songs? In the 21st century? And who needs to know how to figure out which way is north without a compass? There's an app for that. Scouting is definitely not the coolest way a young man could choose to spend his time, and even some of our own scouts were not keen on being seen in public wearing their uniform shirts.

And then when the BSA does make an effort to change with the times – welcoming gay adult leaders or opening the door to female scouts – some of their traditional constituency heads for the door, as did the Mormon contingent at the start of 2020, a loss representing 18 percent of BSA membership. Talk about a rock and a hard place.

As I write this, the BSA has filed for bankruptcy protection as they continue to settle legal actions from the past cases of abuse that have haunted the organization for decades. Lawyers are running televisions ads soliciting victims, and they're finding plenty of clients.

So clearly there have been systemic issues, and the future of scouting is very much in doubt. But here's my two cents: Being a Boy Scout was a great thing for our son, and maybe for your child too. Forget the skits and songs (our group wasn't big on the singing): Scouts learn leadership skills, independence and an appreciation of the outdoors (in other words, long stretches of time when they're not glued to an electronic device), and the fundamentals of being a good citizen are constantly and consistently reinforced.

None of this minimizes in any way the pain of the victims of abuse. Virtually all who have come forward, however, have reported incidents that occurred well before the BSA put its current youth protection measures in place.

As a troop we would annually put our best foot forward for the families of the boys who were completing their time as Cub Scouts, in the hope that they would 'bridge over' to Troop 328. Some families would decide not to continue without giving Boy Scouts a chance, others were all in… and the majority were on the fence. I would try to nudge them in the right direction.

The analogy I often used with the parents of these incoming Cub Scouts was this: If you ever coached a youth sports team, you learned pretty quickly that when you wanted your own child to actually learn something you would send them to one of the other coaches, because kids often tune out Mom or Dad after a while. Scouting is like that other parent, supporting the lessons and values you're teaching at home, another positive voice in your child's ear at a time in their lives when they're hearing many other, less desirable voices.

Consider the 12 points of the Scout Law: A Scout is trustworthy, loyal, helpful, friendly, courteous, kind, obedient, cheerful, thrifty, brave, clean and reverent.

Tell me: Which of those could our world not use more of at the moment?

THE SCOUTMASTER MINUTE

Spoiler alert: The next Scoutmaster of Troop 328 was me, a development that remains surprising to me to this day, for reasons you'll read about in just a moment. First, though, a little background on the structure of this book.

On the day of the funeral service for the Browning family, our troop Committee Chair, Jim, handed me a small paperback published by the BSA, a collection of Scoutmaster Minutes. This is a tradition in Boy Scouts, the idea being that each weekly troop meeting concludes with a brief message from the Scoutmaster, a positive thought to send the boys out the door and into their week with a bit of inspiration or motivation.

Inside the front cover of the book Jim had inscribed a message thanking me for stepping up in the troop's time of need and stating his desire that the troop return to having a weekly Scoutmaster Minute. "This book," he wrote, "is a guide to help you get us back on track."

That last bit was well put, because that was exactly how I used the book: as a guide. I don't think I used more than one or two of the actual entries from it over my five years as Scoutmaster. To be honest, most were kind of dated and hokey.

I did, however, fully embrace the idea of a weekly Scoutmaster Minute, largely because giving a homily to a captive audience was much more up my alley than teaching scout skills like orienteering. This was the one part of the job I felt I could do well, and I worked hard to make it so. Troop 328 once again began concluding its meetings with a Scoutmaster Minute (although if I'm being honest, mine were sometimes known as the Scoutmaster *Five* Minutes).

This ritual became a calling card of my time as Scoutmaster. The material I chose seemed to resonate with the boys, and more than one scout mentioned those Scoutmaster Minutes as a source of inspiration in reflections at his Eagle Scout ceremony. I take a bit of pride in that, because there's a big range of worldview and attention span between an 11-year-old boy and a 17-year-old, and I had to hold the attention of both, as well all those in between. In addition, we were a mix of nationalities and cultures, and we always had at least a handful of boys with attention deficit issues. I like to think that my success in holding the attention of a troop of adolescents in the age of Adderall and smartphones lends some credibility to the advice you'll find about speaking to a group a little further along in this book.

The day after each troop meeting I would write down the Scoutmaster Minute I had delivered the previous evening (I never put them to paper beforehand; more on that later), mostly so I wouldn't repeat ideas. There were recurring themes, but I tried not to do the exact same message twice, with just a few exceptions.

Though you may not be a teenager anymore, and though some of the references to news and popular culture have long since passed their expiration dates, many of the messages resonate at any age, and many make just as much sense in the spheres of business leadership and adult life. From that archive, I'll share some of those Scoutmaster Minutes throughout this book.

Here, then, the story of a Leader by Accident.

Scoutmaster Minute
HOW WILL YOU FEEL IF YOU DON'T?

I heard a story this week that I enjoyed. It was about a lady who thought it would be a good idea to go bungee jumping… at least she thought it was a good idea until she got up on the bridge, 150 feet above a pond. Then, understandably, she froze, and it took several tries before they could talk her into jumping.

Afterwards, another member of her group who had jumped before her asked: "Tell me, what was it they said to you up there that made you finally jump?" She replied, "They only said two things: 'Imagine how you'll feel after you do this… *and imagine how you'll feel if you don't.*'"

You guys are at a place in your lives where you have lots of opportunities to try new things. Most of them won't be as scary as jumping off a bridge, but there's fear in trying anything new: trying out for a sports team, auditioning for a show, maybe being a leader in your Scout troop for the first time.

1

When an opportunity to try something new comes up, there are two voices in your head. One says, "Why not? This might be fun; maybe I'll be good at it." The other one says, "I'm not going to be any good at this; I'll feel stupid; I'll embarrass myself." You need to listen to that first voice, because here's the thing: If you go into something new believing that you're going to fail, *you'll be right every single time.*

When you have the chance to try something new, remember the lady who bungee-jumped and *imagine how you'll feel if you don't.*

THE FIRST DAYS

On that same Sunday that the news of the Browning tragedy broke, I suggested to our son Matt that he and I take a walk on what was a reasonably nice day for February. Matt was 12, and as parents we were naturally concerned about the immediate effects of the news on him. I had no answers, but I thought moving our legs and our lips at the same time might be therapeutic. Probably the best thing you could say about my parenting skills in that moment would be that I didn't *pretend* to have any answers. I remember saying to him, "Bud, I have no idea what to tell you about this." And I remember that that was ok. We walked and talked about completely unrelated things, and maybe it helped.

That evening, we returned from an extremely subdued Super Bowl gathering just in time for a phone call from Jim, chairman of the Troop Committee. A Boy Scout troop, like so many other organizations, is guided by a committee of adults who have the ultimate say in how things are run. The Scoutmaster runs the troop activities (with a lot of help), but serves at the pleasure of the committee.

Jim advised me that he had made arrangements to have grief counselors on hand for the boys at the weekly troop meeting the following evening, a forward-thinking gesture for which I still give him much credit. He then noted that at the adults' committee meeting on Tuesday, Item Number One on the agenda would be choosing a new Scoutmaster.

And he added, "Your name has come up."

There was nothing at all funny about the situation, but I think I chuckled and said something along the lines of, "I'm sure you're mistaken," because I figured the stress of the day had gotten to Jim and he had gotten his phone calls mixed up.

I thought this for several reasons: As a young man, I myself had been a Boy Scout for all of about two weeks (didn't like it). I had no outdoor skills or other scouting qualifications to speak of. And we as a family had been involved in the troop for less than two years to that point. In short, I was utterly unqualified.

While I had volunteered to help out on a couple of camping trips, and had helped to organize a couple more, I didn't have a position in the troop and—if I'm being honest—didn't want one. So I was certain that I was not going to be the one to step into the oversized and suddenly empty Scoutmaster shoes of John Browning.

On Monday evening we gathered for the regular weekly troop meeting, except of course that there was nothing regular about it. To this day, it's hard for me to think about that night without a knot in my stomach and tears in my eyes. The raw emotion and grief in that room were like nothing I had ever experienced. Tears, hugs and more tears… from Scouts and adults alike.

While the boys were in their discussions with the grief counselors, the adults attempted to conduct at least a bit of troop business on the fringes of the meeting, and it gradually became clear to me that Jim was not kidding when he had called the night before: not only was I on the short list to be the new Scoutmaster, I'm pretty sure I *was* the short list. It was mystifying to me, but the maelstrom of emotion that night was such that it swept everything else to the side.

As I mentioned, our troop meetings ended with the Scouts forming a circle for final announcements. I could see that a couple of adults were addressing the scouts as they stood in their circle, and I heard the grief counselors promise to be available for any needed follow-up. And then something remarkable happened.

Ryan was then the troop's senior patrol leader, which is similar to being a team captain in a sport. More to the point, Ryan and his family were closer to the Brownings than anyone, and he must have been feeling as though he'd lost two of his own brothers that night. No one would have blamed him if he had skipped the meeting, but he took his leadership role very seriously.

(I later found out that Ryan also had a bit of an inside scoop from his dad at this point that I was likely to be the next Scoutmaster. Sometimes you truly are the last to know.)

In any event, as I walked past the circle of scouts, Ryan opened a space and said, "Mr. Rafferty, do you want to say anything?"

When I recall that moment, I think about all the stories we've heard over the years of people doing remarkable things in stressful circumstances. I had not given a moment's thought to saying anything to the group, and to this day I don't know why I accepted or where the words came from, but I stepped into the circle and said:

"Guys, you've had a lot of good help here tonight. The counselors have listened and talked with you and everyone has said they're here for you any time you have questions. But the question you have is the one we all have, and it's the one we can't answer: '*Why?* Why can something like this happen?' I don't know; no one does. But I promise you this:

You will not go through this alone. Look around this circle at your fellow Scouts and every single adult and know that we are here for you. Anytime you need to talk, cry, scream or share whatever you're feeling, you reach out to any one of us at any time and we'll be there. We will get through this by being there for each other."

We adjourned the meeting, hugged each other and sniffled our way out of the church hall.

The next evening went as predicted and I found myself on the receiving end of a full-court press to accept the Scoutmaster position. Three other dads who were all far more qualified said they would be happy to serve as assistants but just couldn't handle the time commitment of the Scoutmaster's job.

When it became obvious that there really was no Plan B, I finally said, "Folks, there are 12 people in this room, and 11 of them have more scouting experience than I do. So, I'm just a bit puzzled by all this. But if you all truly feel that this is the best thing for the troop right now, so be it. I'll accept the position."

That decision ranks right behind asking my wife to marry me all those years ago as the best, most life-changing thing I've ever done. The five years that followed were an unbroken string of adventures and learning experiences, and they were challenging and rewarding in ways that I will struggle to put to paper.

More to the point, those years as Scoutmaster changed me in fundamental ways, opened my eyes to new possibilities, and taught real-world lessons that I still reflect upon today, lessons that I hope will have meaning for you as well. Taking on that leadership role reshaped me in ways that would prove invaluable just a few years later when I reached the next watershed moment in my life.

How would I feel if I hadn't said yes? I can't imagine.

Scoutmaster Minute
WHEN ARE YOU A SCOUT?

When are you a Scout? *(The Scouts answer: "all the time," "24/7," etc.)*

That's right, the Scout Oath says "to help other people at all times," not just when you're in uniform or when you're camping.

So how do we act like a Scout? The answer is in a lot of small decisions you make every day. Some of them you probably do without even thinking about it: "I'm going to stand here for a few extra seconds and hold the door open for the kid behind me who's carrying his band instrument and his science project." Some of those decisions require a little more effort: When my mom asks me to do something, do I immediately pause Guitar Hero and go do it, or do I give her a lot of backtalk about how it's not my turn, why do I always have to do that, and so on? And some take a little more courage: When my friends are making fun of the uncoordinated kid in gym class, do I join in with them, or do I say, "Hey, guys, leave him alone." (As someone who was that uncoordinated kid, I hope you choose the second one).

The point is that acting like a Scout isn't something that takes more of your time, and it's not something to add to your 'to-do' list. It's right there in the decisions you make every day. Take a minute at the end of the day and think about how you did… give yourself credit for the ones you got right, and if you could have done better, think about how you'll handle that situation next time.

THE FIRST WEEK

That was the very first Scoutmaster Minute Troop 328 heard from me, and it came following a week that could only be described as "dizzying." When I accepted the Scoutmaster position, the Browning family funeral service was just a few days away and looming as a major media event, so there would be no easing into things. Obviously, none of us had ever been through anything like this, and we had no idea what the long-term impact on the troop would be, or if it could even survive such a tragedy.

The morning after I became Scoutmaster I sat and composed a lengthy email to the troop's parents. The people in the meeting the night before represented only a portion of the families involved, so I wanted to be very transparent about what had happened behind those closed doors.

In the note, I acknowledged our collective pain and the healing process that lay ahead. I frankly addressed my own scouting inexperience and pointed out that other, more qualified hands would be assisting and guiding me going forward, and I called on every parent to do the same: to find a way to get involved and help the troop.

And do you know what? They did. Responses began coming back with offers of help in nearly every facet of the troop's operations, and the vast majority followed through.

One of the goals in Scouting is that of the "boy-led" troop, an ideal situation where the Scouts themselves organize and plan troop activities. In practice, it takes some adult guidance, and it truly does take a village of adults to run point on things like the troop's finances, the mountains of paperwork and the logistics of transportation to and from camping weekends and other events—and the endless permission forms.

That was perhaps my first leadership lesson as Scoutmaster: Sometimes you just have to ask.

That initial email generated a number of replies, most of the "thank you for stepping up" variety, but one in particular meant a lot to me. It came from another troop dad whom I had come to know and respect greatly. Fred was president of a large, local defense contracting firm (and months away from being kicked upstairs to COO of their new parent corporation). Clearly he knew a thing or two about leadership. About my admission that I was unqualified for the job he said, "…right now the most important qualifications are leadership and heart, and you're fully qualified there."

Knowing that someone like that was in my corner made me begin to feel that this might just work out.

◆——————◆

Later that day, we learned that protesters from Westboro Baptist Church planned to demonstrate at the funeral. You may recall the fine folks of Westboro, who somehow manage to connect imaginary dots between the deaths of American soldiers abroad and God's purported hatred of homosexuals. I consider myself pretty tolerant of religious viewpoints that differ from my own, but if the elevator pitch for your faith involves the word "hate," it's probably time to find a different one. Knowing that these publicity-seekers wanted to pile on and make this horrific week even worse made me seethe… which of course was exactly their intent.

In any event, their planned presence had very little to do with what had actually transpired and everything to do with the fact that TV cameras would be present. Their plans became known to one of the Assistant Scoutmasters, and the four of us agreed to keep it to ourselves for the time being so as not to spook the parental herd, so to speak, and add further trauma to a week that had provided more than enough already.

A few calls were made and by the next day a resolution was achieved: An assembly permit that would supersede any other permits (including Westboro's) had been issued by Baltimore County for the funeral. In short, they would not be allowed on the church property. Problem solved.

Problem solved, that is, until word leaked a little further and a parent fired off a panicky email to *all* the troop families alerting them to Westboro's plans. Despite our best efforts the herd had indeed been spooked. Given no choice, I had to respond to all to let them know we were aware and that the situation had been dealt with to the best of our abilities. Crisis (sort of) averted.

So it was a great first couple of days on the job.

The happy ending, such as it was: When Saturday and the service rolled around, the Westboro folks found themselves banished to an area across the street from the rear of the church. Even better, someone cleverly decided that that particular stretch of road would be the perfect place to park all the school buses bringing groups to the service, providing a ready-made visual barrier. And best of all, the protesters found themselves pretty much ignored by the TV cameras. The funeral service proceeded without incident.

◆————————◆

Things to smile about were few and far between that week, but one arrived in the form of an unexpected package from Amazon. It was courtesy of a few of the leaders of our scouting district as a thank-you-and-good-luck present. In the box was a DVD of a long-forgotten Disney movie called *Follow Me, Boys!* starring Fred MacMurray as another unwitting Scoutmaster and a very young Kurt Russell as his biggest challenge. To the best of my knowledge, it remains the only movie ever made about the Boy Scouts. It's cheesier than a deep-dish pizza, and wonderful, and in that particular week it was the perfect diversion.

◆————————◆

The funeral service took place at around midday in a massive, newly constructed mega-church that barely contained the mourners. John and Tammy had been very active not only in scouting but in the PTA, recreational sports in the community... you name it, they were there, and the packed house reflected the wide and deep impact they had made on our community.

The troop gathered in the vestibule beforehand to go over how we would line up and process in to our reserved seating area. Before the start, I asked the boys to circle up, thanked them for taking pains to have their uniforms looking great, and told them I was proud to be their Scoutmaster. We would make it through this day and whatever came after it as a group, I said, continuing the theme of the week.

Of the service itself I remember only fragments: Ryan and his dad Lee (now an Assistant Scoutmaster) giving eulogies that were moving and heartfelt and somehow delivered dry-eyed, which was more than I could have managed. The scouts filing in and out, in full dress uniform with chins up and looking as numb as we all felt. And a young lady with a guitar singing an aching rendition of Sarah McLachlan's "Angel," the memory of which threatens tears even now.

Then it was over, and I don't think anyone accomplished much the rest of that day.

A Scout is brave.

When we hear that word, we think about someone pulling people out of a burning building or rescuing someone from raging floodwaters... but most of our chances to be brave won't ever make the newspapers.

We talked a couple of weeks ago about standing up to your friends when they're making fun of someone else or doing anything wrong. There's a reason it's called peer *pressure*, and there's going to come a time (if it hasn't already) when you'll be with a group of people who decide to do something you know is not right. It takes courage to do the right thing.

It takes courage to call a girl on the phone and ask her out to a movie; and it takes courage to knock on a door and ask someone if they'd like to buy something to support your Boy Scout troop.

Being brave doesn't mean the *absence of fear*; it means looking that fear in the eye and deciding you're bigger than it. The worst that girl can do is laugh at you for asking her out. And if she does, you probably didn't want to go out with her anyway. The worst someone can do when you knock on their door is to say, "No, thanks," and then you're no worse off than you were before you knocked.

Not only are you no worse off, you're better off... because you know you identified your fear and you conquered it. That's how a Scout is brave.

COMFORT ZONE

Much has been said and written in the world of business and self-help literature about getting out of your comfort zone. More will be said here, because I now consider myself something of an expert on the topic.

Accepting a demanding and time-consuming volunteer job like Scoutmaster of a Boy Scout troop qualifies as stepping out of your comfort zone under any circumstances, I believe. Accepting a demanding and time-consuming volunteer job for which you have no qualifications is perhaps a bigger step. And accepting a demanding and time-consuming volunteer job for which you have no qualifications at a time when the organization has just endured an unimaginable tragedy, casting its future into doubt... well, that's maybe more of a leap than a step. And a leap it was.

Beyond the virtual discomfort of a new set of responsibilities, though, I was about to learn in very literal ways what it meant to get out of your comfort zone, because that's what Scouting does.

Over those next five years, we spent our weekends camping, hiking, bicycling, canoeing, sledding, boating, kayaking and climbing in the heat, cold, rain, snow and wind. And all that was just the warm-up for a couple of "high adventure" trips for the older Scouts.

In 2009, we traveled to the Sea Base Scout reservation in the lower Florida Keys. Our week there involved rowing *Hawaii Five-O* style war canoes about 4½ miles out to a little speck of an island, quite the workout. That island was the jumping-off point for five days of camping, fishing, kayaking, snorkeling (day and night) and shark-feeding (on purpose). We had one set each of "wet clothes" and "dry clothes" and not nearly enough Gold Bond powder to bridge the gap between the two, and by the end of the week the remaining Gold Bond was the subject of many carefully-considered barter transactions between the Scouts, who had learned firsthand the scourge of crotch rot.

We had not only no phones, but no watches, no electronics of any kind, nothing electric except our flashlights. Imagine spending the better part of a week never once knowing what time it was. What a luxury.

And, oh yes, all this happened in July. In southernmost Florida. So at night the temperatures dropped to about 85 degrees... outside our tents. Unfortunately, we were *inside* our tents.

On the first night, our son Matt and his tentmate Kenny, who were both pretty large fellows for their age, didn't realize there was a zippered ventilation flap at the *back* of their tent as well as the front. Said flap remained tightly closed and they spent the night roasting like two Butterball turkeys. They figured it out the next day, when they were each about five pounds lighter.

Even with both flaps open it was very still and *very* tropical. I was fortunate enough to have a tent to myself, and I remember trying to sleep through the sensation of individual rivulets of sweat breaking free and rolling down through various bodily areas. Then one night I realized that one of those sweat droplets was moving *uphill*, which even in my sleep-deprived state didn't seem quite right. I waited a moment and again felt a gravity-defying tickle and decided it was time to investigate, at which point I discovered that a sand crab had taken up residence in the crotch of my shorts. As I also happened to be occupying those shorts at the time, this was unnerving, to say the least. This incident remains at the top of my list of ways I never want to be woken up again.

We all had a unique lesson in leaving our comfort zones when snorkeling night arrived. If you've never snorkeled in the dark, it's a pretty interesting experience. Set this book down for a moment and do this: close one eye, then curl your hand into a little telescope shape and look through it with the other eye. (If you're sitting in a public place as you read this, just use your imagination.)

That limited field of vision will begin to give you an idea of the sensation of being underwater at night, because outside the beam of your flashlight, all is blackness. All is silence also, except for the theme from *Jaws* going through your head (ba-*dumm*... ba-*dumm*...). In other words, it's more than a little creepy even before you see a barracuda or shark gliding through the periphery of your limited vision. Which you will, if you're in the Keys.

So it wasn't too surprising that while the scouts were very excited about the *idea* of snorkeling at night, they found the reality much less charming, and most were back in our boats after less than ten minutes. Those boats were actually long canoes joined in pairs side by side, leaving a gap of perhaps three feet between the two.

As the number of people in the water dwindled, I snorkeled around for a bit longer and then finally headed back toward my own crew's canoes. Surfacing at a bit of a distance, I could see that by now all the boys had thought better of the idea and were sitting there waiting for their adult leaders to return so we could start paddling back to the island. And at that point I got a slightly fiendish idea. I decided it would be good, clean fun to startle the scouts a little by popping out of the water in that space between the two canoes.

I switched off my flashlight so they wouldn't see me coming, quietly swam close enough to cover the remaining distance in one breath and then dove, swimming underwater until I was directly beneath the gap between the boats. Then I launched myself upwards, kicking my flippers to power towards the surface.

This would have been fine if not for the fact that at that very moment one of my scouts decided for reasons unknown to lean over and peer downward into that same dark gap. Ian had barely craned his neck over the side of the canoe when I exploded out of the water, inches from his face.

Ian was and is a very tall and sturdy fellow, yet somehow he actually managed to levitate several inches off his seat. And I would guess that the echoes of his scream are still reverberating somewhere down there among the mangroves. Needless to say, it wasn't my finest moment as a leader... it seems that horrifying your charges is generally frowned upon. I only hope Ian's not still telling the story to his therapist.

◆————————◆

Another high adventure trip took us to Yellowstone National Park, where we spent a July week backpacking through the southwest corner of the massive park under postcard-perfect skies. Unfortunately, the ground beneath our feet didn't get the memo. It had been a big year for snow, and the ensuing spring melt had swollen the many streams and rivers of Yellowstone to the point where we had to change our itinerary because they couldn't be forded to get to some of the campsites we were supposed to occupy.

We spent most of our week crisscrossing an area called The Meadows, which I guess was a technically accurate name except that *these* meadows were largely underneath 6 to 12 inches of water at that point. I gave up on wearing my boots after day one and wound up putting about 27 miles on a pair of hiking sandals, which were not nearly as kind to my feet. The blisters took a few weeks to heal.

Whenever we were outside our tents we were sure to have netting over our hats and heads, and to regularly rub our arms and legs down with DEET, because another byproduct of the wet conditions was a bumper crop of mosquitoes. The soundtrack to that week was the constant whine of the cloud of skeeters that surrounded each of us, all the time, as though we were always 5 miles away from a NASCAR race.

How bad were the mosquitoes? One of our Assistant Scoutmasters, Mike, was sharing a tent with his son William that week. They woke up one morning wondering what time it might be, because it felt too late to be as dark outside as it was. Then one of them whacked the roof panel of their tent from inside and the mosquitoes that had been shoulder to shoulder, literally blotting out the light, flew off. *Voila!* Just like that, it was morning.

For the capper on that trip, on our last day in the park we forded a river that was almost chest-deep (on me, at six-foot-four) with a water temperature of about 50 degrees. At 9 o'clock in the morning. In other words, it was something like the polar opposite (pun intended) of our sweltering week in the Keys.

◆────────◆

A third high-adventure outing had nothing to do with scouting: In 2010, my wife Monica and I and our friends Anthony and Donna backpacked to the bottom of the Grand Canyon and spent four nights there in various campsites.

Now, when I say we hiked down and back I don't mean on the nice, flat, wide trail the mules use. Ours was among the more rugged backcountry approaches, and involved climbing over boulders much larger than we were. And we tried not to look down as we clambered over them, because many of those rocks appeared to be perched on the edge of the world... it was a *long* way down. Monica being an even less experienced hiker than I was, and carrying 30-plus pounds on her 5-foot-1 frame, it was a slow and difficult trip down, physically and mentally. We reached our campsite some nine hours after we started.

I vividly remember that first evening. After we got our tents set up and got settled, we all sat for a bit resting and reflecting. I looked off in the general direction I knew we had come from and pointed at the highest spot I could see, which was unimaginably far away. I said, "That's where we started, right?" And Anthony, who'd organized the trip, shook his head, smiled ruefully and said, "No, it's higher than that. You can't see it from here."

Higher than that? *I'm going to die down here*, I thought, *because there's just no way.*

The first 24 hours in the canyon were so difficult emotionally, with the specter of making that return trip looming over our every moment. There were many tears (from Monica, too). Anthony and Donna, who had done a similar trip before, showed great patience with us two rookies, though they must have been wondering what possessed them to invite us in the first place.

And then we adjusted. Physically, we got more comfortable with our packs, and mentally, we moved forward into "suck it up, buttercup" mode. The impossible started to feel possible and we managed to actually relax and enjoy amazing scenery in places that very few humans ever visit.

We camped one night on the banks of the Colorado River with rushing Class 5 rapids as the white noise for our sleep (and took a bracing dip that day in the 55-degree water). The next day was a study in contrasts as we hiked up and away from the river to our next campsite. At one point, Anthony noted that the site was only another mile away, and we all thought "great, a pretty easy day."

What he failed to mention was that that mile had 800 feet of elevation change in it, all uphill. It was beyond taxing, and our reward was arriving at possibly the most desolate spot I've ever seen. The campsite was on a promontory with no shade or shelter of any kind, and no water source. We rigged a tent fly to keep the midday sun off us and stretched out for a nap, sure that we would awaken to circling buzzards. (Later in the day, we made a group decision to violate our camping permit and backtrack to another site we had passed. It was cool, shaded and had a stream running through it. Don't tell Mr. or Ms. Ranger.)

On Thursday morning we rose before the sun, packed up and started our journey out of the canyon by the same route we'd used to descend. And you know what? Our newfound optimism was well-placed: With gravity against us, we were three hours *faster* going up than we were going down, even with the dreaded Cathedral Stairs as part of the ordeal. The last two and a half miles were a series of switchbacks that seemed never to end, probably the most grueling physical workout I've ever had. My last memory of being in the canyon was passing a guide with a group of schoolchildren. "You're almost there!" she said, with an enthusiasm I didn't share at that moment. And then I reached the rim, the straggler in our foursome.

There a minor miracle awaited us: Back in the parking lot where we'd left the rental car, we discovered that a few leftover beers we'd kept in a Mylar bag with some ice since Sunday morning were *still cold*. That was the best beer of my life, hands down (a Dale's Pale Ale at 11 am, if you were wondering). And it was followed closely by the best (and only) coin-operated shower of my life, because we did not smell so good by that point.

Scoutmaster Minute
THAT FIRST STEP

I am not very experienced at canoeing; our trip on Saturday was my second time out. There's that first moment when you step off the shore and into the canoe, and it always puts a little knot in my stomach: You step into some muck, then into the canoe (which rocks back and forth until you get settled), and then you're out in the river and you don't know what's ahead. There's no way of telling how fast the water is or where the rocks are, and to top it off we had a pretty good chance of some nasty weather when we set out that day.

We have a number of experiences like that in Scouting where you have to take a little leap of faith without knowing what's ahead: going away to Summer Camp for the first time, whitewater rafting, the caving trip we did a couple of years back. That first step into a new adventure can be a little scary.

I think that's one of the great things Scouting gives you: the chance, and the skills and the confidence, to step into the unknown. You're going to have a lot of moments like that in your life: going off to a new school, starting a new job or a new relationship, becoming a Scoutmaster for the first time... there's no way to tell what's around the bend or where the rocks are.

The things you do as a Scout give you the confidence to say, "I don't know exactly what's ahead, but I'm confident enough in my skills and my knowledge to believe that I can handle it."

SO WHAT?

At this point it would be fair of you to ask, "So what, Jim? So you learned to love the outdoors and did some challenging things. What does that have to do with real life, or with me?" It's a reasonable question, and here's the answer:

In 2012, a year of sheer agony at work culminated in the loss of the job I'd held for nearly 21 years. I had spent those two decades as the marketing and sales manager for a well-known local home improvement company. The year before, the owner of the firm, who was getting up there in years, had sold the company to a well-to-do local businessman. It did not go well for me from there, in the same general sense that Little Big Horn did not go well for General Custer.

I can count on one hand (with a few fingers left over) the people I've encountered in my life for whom I harbor bad feelings. Truly, I am not one to hold a grudge. The new owner of the company, however, managed to prove the exception to this rule with a toxic blend of arrogance and incompetence. I was born and bred to be the loyal company soldier, and I kept expecting things to get better, but I was in denial on this one.

Again and again I would suggest doing things a certain way, get ridiculed for it and then watch as this consultant or that one came in and offered the EXACT same advice, which then became gospel. Not once but twice, the new owner hired people who were to report to me... *before I met them.* Choose your word: frustrating, demoralizing, demotivating...

How bad was it? In April of 2012 we executed a new compensation package for me, one I had been trying to get done for some time. It had lower fixed costs for the company and a higher upside for me; in other words, a smaller base salary and more commission. The new owner and I signed it on a Friday afternoon with smiles and a handshake and he said, "I hope you make a ton of money!"

I then went away on a brief, scheduled trip with our son for his first round of college visits, got back into Baltimore the following Thursday and returned to work on Friday morning, exactly one week later... at which point I was threatened with termination because of declining sales results. Besides the fact that we were just a week removed from all the smiles and handshakes, there was one other odd thing about this: Sales weren't declining. My team had *exceeded* all their goals to that point in the year.

Two months later the inevitable happened and He Who Must Not Be Named told me my position would have to be eliminated because of pressure put on him by his lender to reduce costs. It wasn't the first time I'd been fired—my career began in the radio industry, where it's practically a badge of honor—but it was by far the hardest. My wife, Monica, held a couple of part-time jobs, but I was the provider of the bulk of our income, as well as our health insurance, and college was looming on Matt's horizon, with our daughter Megan just a few years behind. Despite the fact that it shouldn't have been a surprise, I was devastated.

As it turned out, he had done me a favor by giving me a head start. In April of the following year, the bank pulled the plug, his wealthy family declined to intervene... and a company that had served Baltimore for more than half a century closed its doors for good.

Numerous homeowners were left with half-completed projects, and countless subcontractors and suppliers were left holding a very large bag of unpaid invoices, money they would never see. Even though I'd already been gone for 10 months, I felt like I'd lost a family member. My 20-plus years at the firm had barely moved me into the top 10 in employee longevity, and to see the brand and reputation we all had spent so much of our lives building destroyed in such short order was heartbreaking.

But back to June of 2012: Armed with some misplaced confidence and six weeks' worth of severance pay to show for my two decades of service, I began to look for a new job, because that was all I knew how to do. I had spent my entire life working for others and had never given a moment's thought to going it on my own. I was a suspenders-and-a-belt kind of guy, and the idea of life without the safety nets of a steady paycheck and health benefits had never been on my radar screen.

There was one small issue with this approach, which I discovered pretty quickly: There didn't seem to be a whole lot of demand for a 51-year-old, self-taught marketer. I had really loved my position because of the variety: I handled the marketing and advertising, managed the sales staff and was the de facto IT guy for a company that didn't have one. There weren't any Help Wanted ads for positions like that, and the diffused focus of my work didn't check off enough boxes for a position in any single one of those disciplines. Jack of All Trades, Master of... Nothing at All.

In fact, the job listings I found generally fell into one of two categories: very corporate-sounding VP/Marketing positions where I would read the listing and think, "I'm pretty sure I could do that, except I don't understand half the jargon in the ad." (Was I cross-functional? Did I know how to leverage consumer insights? Was my experience in a multi-channel environment?)

And in the other type of posting, the words would magically rearrange themselves before my eyes to say, "We need a 23-year-old to do Facebook and Twitter posts, but we can't come out and say that."

And so this was the situation: I was an unemployed middle-aged man with no good prospects. The fairly reasonable health care coverage we'd managed to find excluded my wife because of a pre-existing condition, and our son was now a year away from beginning college we knew not where, but we were pretty sure it would be expensive.

In the middle of this waking nightmare, a friend from Scouting asked me to stop by his local business to talk about his website and marketing. Shortly thereafter, a family member by marriage asked me to look over a proposal he had received from a vendor who wanted to redo his company's website. And then my former boss, who had launched his own home improvement firm, invited me to stop by to talk about his marketing. "Someone is trying to tell me something," I thought.

But here at last is the answer to that "So what?" question that started the chapter, and I believe this in my bones: The old, pre-scouting Jim might have taken on some consulting work, but would have found a way to have the full-time gig and the safety net, too. Consulting would have been side work, and I would have found a job with a steady paycheck, even if it had nothing to do with my experience or my interests. I would have had a job to have a job.

The Jim who'd survived a sand crab in his shorts, managed the shin-deep waters of The Meadows and the relentless mosquitoes of Yellowstone, who had overcome the physical and emotional challenges and managed to haul his middle-aged backside out of the Grand Canyon… that Jim said, "Let's do this." I filed the paperwork that established JMRketing, told the state of Maryland to stop sending the unemployment checks and stepped off the virtual cliff into entrepreneurship.

Eight years later, I can say that however you care to define the term, I am doing better than ever before. My income is higher, my stress is lower, I have almost complete control over my schedule, and for the first six years the biggest issue on my commute to work would be the occasional sleeping cat on the stairs in our center hallway (I now share an office 10 minutes from home). I love my work, which has taken me to places I couldn't have imagined, and I'm proud to say that nearly all of it has come via referrals.

And those three people who reached out to me when I was looking for work? All are still clients. God bless them for lighting the way.

◆——————◆

As noted in that Scoutmaster Minute, in any outdoor adventure, there's an uncertain—and sometimes scary—first step. The first step off the pavement and onto the trail, not knowing what's ahead. The first step into a wobbly canoe when you haven't yet seen what awaits you downstream. The first step onto an airplane, knowing that in the coming week you're responsible for the health and safety of a dozen or more young men in a rugged and dangerous environment.

One of the things that gave me an extra measure of empathy as a Scoutmaster was that those first steps for the boys were often first steps for me, too. And I have absolutely no doubt that all those first steps I took on our scouting adventures added up to the courage to take the first steps into entrepreneurship.

The journey of thousand miles begins with a single step, says the adage. Make it a memorable one. Trust me on this: Whatever is next for you, it begins with taking that first step out of your comfort zone.

There's one more point to be made about all this, and that has to do with the power of a firm belief that things work out for the best. Some, including myself, see the hand of God acting in our lives, while others see karma or the universe at work. One way or another, even in the darkest times, I have always believed that even if I couldn't see my path at that moment, it would appear.

Three different business owners asking me for marketing help within the span of a few weeks of unemployment made for a pretty obvious signpost, but often the light on the path is more subtle.

As I was living through it, I found very few positives in my year of frustration and marginalization at the hands of a consultant-obsessed boss. But throughout all that misery, I was paying attention: I watched how all those consultants conducted themselves in ways good and bad; I noticed the ones who went out of their way to get to know the rest of the staff and saw how much easier that made things for them; and I developed a pretty good understanding of how much they charged for their services.

Paying attention to what was going around me during that year of misery gave me a major leg up when the time came to hang out my own shingle. I was able to avoid a lot of rookie mistakes, and to look a business owner in the eye when I quoted my rates, knowing that even though it seemed like a lot of money to me, I was right in line with what the market would bear.

It's easy to find the lesson when it's painted on a signpost for us, but it can take a little more work and reflection, and usually some time as well, to understand the meaning in our suffering.

Scoutmaster Minute
DON'T SAY NO

Back in 1973, Tony was a teenager finishing up his third year of riding the bench for his school basketball team. The coach, who was also the baseball coach, had also discouraged Tony from coming out for the baseball team in the spring because he didn't want him to go through the heartache of being cut. So Tony was not in a happy place at that point; he really wanted to be an athlete, and it didn't look like things were going to work out that way.

One Saturday, Tony's doorbell rang and he answered to find his neighbor, a man in his 50s, standing there. Tony turned to get his parents, but his neighbor said, "I'm not here to see your parents; I'm here to see you. I was about to go out for a run and I wondered if you'd like to join me." Now remember, this was 1973; running was not the popular recreational pastime it is now. You didn't see people jogging all over the neighborhood like you do today.

Tony really didn't want to go, but something made him say "yes," and he and his neighbor went up to the high school track where the neighbor timed him while he ran a mile... in 8 minutes, not too bad for his first time out.

By sheer coincidence, when Tony went back to school on Monday, the track coach spotted him in the hallway and said, "Tony, there's a track meet tomorrow. How would you like to run the mile?" Again, Tony said "yes"... and finished dead last.

To cut to the chase: Tony Schiller became one of America's top distance runners. He won 17 triathlons and five world titles and was still competing against young guys when he was in his late 40s. But here's what I think is the most impressive statistic: He ran in over 600 distance events and finished every single one.

Now, there are two points to this story: First, God bless the neighbor for going out of his way just a little bit and taking an interest in someone else, because it literally changed a life.

But the other point is this: Tony had a chance to try something new and he *didn't say no*. He not only gave it a try, he stuck with it even when he didn't succeed at first.

You may or may not ever have a single life-changing moment like Tony did. But I do know this: If you do, no one is going to tap you on the shoulder and say, "Here it is! Your life-changing moment is here!" You only realize that afterwards. So keep an open mind, and don't be afraid of trying new things... be afraid of the opportunity you might miss if you don't.

YOUR COMFORT ZONE

I f you've ever served in the military, or even if you're simply an avid outdoorsperson, I imagine you've been chuckling your way through the last couple of chapters as I've described the mild discomfort on our camping adventures that took me out of my comfort zone. It's hardly the stuff of Navy SEAL training, or even "Naked and Afraid."

On the other hand, some of the things I've done pretty routinely, like singing as a soloist in front of a church full of 500 people or speaking to thousands as a radio announcer, well… those might put your antiperspirant to the test. I've often said I would rather be on a stage in front of a room packed with people than standing with two strangers at a networking event. Making small talk is outside my comfort zone (so I'm working on it).

And that is exactly the point: Your comfort zone and mine are probably different. While I think the adventures I've described here would challenge most people, they might constitute just another weekend for you.

The bottom line is to do *something*. The act of facing down the things that make you uncomfortable—whatever they are—allows you to grow, and if we're not growing, well… why bother?

Let's look at the individual components of my experience:

The Outdoors: If you never, ever want to spend a night in a tent, so be it. I highly recommend it, but maybe your idea of roughing it is a second-floor motel room. Let me suggest that you at least get out for a walk in the woods, or on a quiet beach or somewhere away from people and buildings, and do it on a regular basis. I do my very best thinking when I'm hiking, concentrating on a completely different level than when I'm pressed for time and just walking around the neighborhood distracted by passing cars and barking dogs.

And no excuses if you're an urbanite: I live 10 minutes from the Baltimore city line, and in less than another five minutes I can be in the woods. Your mileage may vary, but I'm sure you can get lost somewhere in your own vicinity. Google "hiking near me" or "trails near me."

If you do choose to challenge yourself with more rigorous adventures like heading into the woods carrying your belongings on your back, you'll find an even greater sense of well-being and accomplishment. There's nothing like doing without some of the conveniences we take for granted to make you not take them for granted anymore.

Volunteering: Wait, what? There's nothing scary about volunteering. Or is there? Probably the most challenging thing here is the same thought I had when they asked me to take on the Scoutmaster role: "Where will I find the time?" We have jobs and kids and responsibilities, and our time is our most precious commodity.

Which is why it feels so good to give it. And if you do have kids, they come fully equipped with unlimited volunteer opportunities from PTA to Scouts to any number of sports teams. I coached or assistant-coached baseball, softball and soccer for both of our children. There were times when I could barely manage to give the hours, but I was always glad I had.

Side benefits include meeting some great new people—and a few challenging ones—and continuing to learn and grow. Volunteering makes you feel better about yourself, and feeling better about yourself makes you better at whatever you do to pay the bills, no doubt about it.

Leadership: To bastardize the Shakespearean quote about greatness, some people are born leaders, some achieve leadership skills and some have leadership thrust upon them. The second and third categories applied to me. The Scoutmaster job certainly was thrust upon me, and I like to think that I achieved some leadership skills along the way.

There are many, many definitions of leadership, nearly as many leadership books, and I'll have more to say about that shortly, but in terms of getting out of your comfort zone, this is the ultimate prescription: Volunteering is a great start, but *leading* a volunteer effort is exponentially better. Raise your hand and take on a leadership position outside of work: Chair your neighborhood committee, coach a team, spearhead a pledge drive for a good cause. You will accrue confidence, and it will absolutely make a difference in your professional life.

If you still doubt that, consider this story from author Kurt Vonnegut, found all over the internet:

When I was 15, I spent a month working on an archeological dig. I was talking to one of the archeologists one day during our lunch break and he asked those kinds of 'getting to know you' questions you ask young people: Do you play sports? What's your favorite subject? And I told him, no I don't play any sports. I do theater, I'm in choir, I play the violin and piano, I used to take art classes. And he went "WOW. That's amazing!"

And I said, "Oh no, but I'm not any good at ANY of them."

And he said something then that I will never forget and which absolutely blew my mind because no one had ever said anything like it to me before: "I don't think being good at things is the point of doing them. I think you've got all these wonderful experiences with different skills, and that all teaches you things and makes you an interesting person, no matter how well you do them."

And that honestly changed my life. Because I went from a failure, someone who hadn't been talented enough at anything to excel, to someone who did things because I enjoyed them. I had been raised in such an achievement-oriented environment, so inundated with the myth of Talent, that I thought it was only worth doing things if you could 'Win' at them.

It's okay to not be the best at something. The simple act of trying new things will make you better at the things you already do.

◆——————◆

In that summer of 2012 when I was still at loose ends, not having decided just yet to give entrepreneurship a try, I started thinking about how I'd really *like* to earn a living, because that's what you do when you're on the cusp of a new chapter in your life. This led to lovely, pessimistic conversations with myself that went like this:

"I like to write." *Writers don't make any money.*

"I really enjoy working with websites." *No one's going to hire you as a web developer.*

"I could do voice-over work." *It would take too long to build enough of a client base to make a living.*

And so on. After many rounds of this set-'em-up-and-knock-'em-down routine, I decided to go the consulting route, and then some interesting things happened.

In my early days of entrepreneurship, when the days were far longer than the to-do list, I heard from my sister-in-law, Cynthia. She worked for a company in the Philadelphia suburbs that produces corporate training study materials and tests, and she wanted to know if I would be interested in writing some multiple-choice questions for them.

Let me check my schedule, I thought. *Hmm… free this week, free next week… sure.*

So I agreed, and they sent the instructions for writing these questions… a 38-page Word document. You read that right: 38 pages on how and how not to write multiple-choice questions. *This,* I thought, *isn't really what I had in mind with the whole marketing thing.*

But I didn't say no.

After I completed a couple assignments, they asked if I would like to come up for a visit and meet some of the people I'd been corresponding with. Again, my dance card had some room, so I took a day and went to Philly, where I was introduced all around to a very nice team.

In the course of that visit, one of the managers asked me if I would send a resume, which I found an odd request since I was just doing some freelance work.

But I didn't say no.

Two things happened after I shared that resume: First, they invited me to interview for a VP/Marketing position. Okay, you've got me there: I *did* say no to that one, strictly because we had kids finishing high school and starting college and were not at a place in our family life where we could consider relocating.

The other thing that happened was this: The same manager noticed my radio background on that resume. And it turned out that the company not only writes training materials, they *record* them and offer them in audio format. He passed my resume to the right person, and several months later, I started doing narration work for them in my home studio (which sounds much more professional than "my old iMac with a nice microphone attached to it and a packing blanket hanging from the basement ceiling to deaden the sound").

Six-plus years later, I could not begin to estimate how many pages or hours of recorded material I've produced for them, or how many multiple-choice questions. But I do know that the combination of the two was a big help in putting two kids through college. Thank you, Cynthia.

And lo and behold, these days I build and tinker with websites, I do a ton of writing, and I do some voice-over work. In other words, that ideal job that didn't exist in 2012? I'm living it. It built itself around me.

Because I didn't say no.

Scoutmaster Minute
GET OUTSIDE

This (springtime) is my favorite time of year… everything is turning green, the trees are flowering, there's nice weather (when it's not pouring rain). But except for the holidays, it's also probably the busiest time of year. Your house is probably a lot like ours, where you come home from school, try to get some homework done and go running back out the door to sports or Scouts or whatever's happening that night.

So tonight, just a suggestion… try to set a few minutes aside every day or two to enjoy the sights and sounds and smells outside. Go climb a tree in the backyard and just sit for a few minutes, or step outside after dark and take a look at the sky. It won't happen by accident… you need to make an effort to set aside the time. Don't be so busy that you forget to enjoy the outdoors.

SOLITUDE

Earlier, I mentioned our mosquito-ridden trip to Yellowstone National Park as an example of getting out of my comfort zone. And so it was, but it was not without its magical moments.

Day One of that trip was a *very* long day. We had spent the night at a base camp in Jackson, Wyoming and departed at around dawn for the 3½ hour ride to the park entrance (probably not the one you used if you've been to Yellowstone... this was a hikers-only entry at the southwest corner of the park). By the time we got there, got all our gear prepared and were ready to hit the trail, it was almost midday. And that 3½ hour ride was in an old-fashioned yellow school bus with leg room meant for elementary school kids, so our discomfort was well underway before we got to the actual hiking.

About 50 yards into the woods we realized the full extent of the skeeter onslaught and took a pause so everyone could grab their mosquito netting out of their packs and put it on. Then we logged about 8 miles that first afternoon. We were a large enough group that we were divided into two crews, because most of the campsites weren't big enough to hold all of us; we hiked together during the day, but on all but the final night we camped separately.

That first night, my crew drew the campsite that was *another* mile along the trail, uphill of course, from the first crew's site. We would backtrack in the morning to meet up with them. We found our campsite and got set up, then the boys went on a little explore and found a natural hot tub along the stream that ran near our site (there are many such features in Yellowstone, thanks to all the volcanic activity). So everyone got a little down time in after a long and grueling day.

Everything was great until we started to prepare dinner and to refill our water bottles for the next day. Each crew had a manual pump to filter the stream and river water so we could safely drink it, and ours chose that moment to break. Predictably, the other crew had the spare.

I volunteered to hike back to their campsite to retrieve the backup pump after dinner since everyone was pretty exhausted (me too, but a leader needs to take one for the team now and again). And so I set out, with maybe an hour of daylight remaining.

A little over a mile in each direction is not that far, but consider this: When was the last time you were at least a half mile from another human being? I will always struggle to describe the feeling of solitude on that brief trek. No people, no traffic noises, no airplanes overhead… just myself and my breathing, a striking landscape and a beautiful sunset, served with a light garnish of fear that a grizzly bear would appear suddenly and eat me.

I'd love to tell you that that moment brought with it a life-changing epiphany or some transformative change. It didn't have to, though, because that sense of solitude by itself was so palpable that I can still recall it all these years later, like nothing else before or since.

The 1981 film Chariots of Fire chronicled the story of two runners from Great Britain preparing for the 1924 Olympic Games. It's a marvelous movie, and the deserving winner of the Academy Award for Best Picture that year.

There's a scene near the start of the film where main character Eric Liddell, known as the Flying Scot, is shown at home in Scotland, leaving Sunday church services and strolling through the heather with his sister. She begins to chide him about giving up this silly business of running and getting on with his life's work as a missionary, which surely is what God has planned for him.

He turns to her and says, "Yes, but God also made me *fast*. And when I run, *I feel His pleasure*."[1]

I fell in love with that line because it acknowledges an extra dimension that reaches beyond our own happiness: It's a different thing altogether to sense that what we're doing makes *the world around us* happy. Some of us may feel God's pleasure in certain moments; others, perhaps a sense that the universe is at one with us and vice versa as we vibrate in unison. Whichever you choose, that's what I felt in those moments of solitude.

To be sure, we don't need to stand in the middle of nowhere to "feel His pleasure." There are other events in our lives when we can feel that sense of completeness, from mountaintop moments like a wedding or the birth of a child to more pedestrian pursuits like being part of a sports team or musical group when everything clicks and the result reaches a new level.

I felt His pleasure in that moment of aloneness, and I'll probably never be able to duplicate it. If you live in an urban area as I do, you probably won't either. But it's so important that we try. The intervening years have brought a geometric increase in the electronic intrusions in our lives. Your mileage may vary if you're not a marketing consultant,

---

1   Chariots of Fire, Directed by Hugh Hudson, 1981, Twentieth Century Fox.

but my phone chimes all day long with notifications from three different email accounts and innumerable social media notices, not to mention the incessant spam and fraud robocalls.

It's harder and harder to find the time and space to think and reflect, and more important than ever that we make the effort.

Good things happen when we give ourselves the space and solitude that the world conspires to deny us. But this doesn't happen by accident; we need to schedule our down time to remove ourselves from the chaos as best we can.

When do you feel His pleasure, or simply feel the pleasure of the world around you? Do more of that. And if you're stuck for an answer, you need to try some new things.

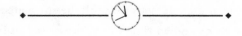

Scoutmaster Minute
ENJOY THE JOURNEY

We were on our canoe trip two weeks ago (and somebody messed up, because we actually had good weather), traveling back to the campsite on Saturday afternoon, and it was just a beautiful drive. The weather was spectacular and the scenery was great, and it occurred to me that one of my favorite things about our trips is not just the canoeing or hiking or whatever we do when we get there, but the getting there. We get to see some really beautiful places, so the small message tonight is to put down the video game player and look out the window once in a while.

We can take that same thought and apply it to your life: We're always in a hurry to get to the next thing, the next milestone. I'll bet most of you can tell me exactly how many days are left in the school year because you can't wait for summer vacation to start. Maybe you can't wait until you're done with your requirements for Eagle Scout so you can put all that Scouting work behind you; or maybe you can't wait until you're 16 so you can drive.

That's all fine; we need to have goals to work toward.

But here's the thing: That milestone, whether it's the last day of school, your Eagle ceremony or whatever, will only take a fraction of the time that all the work to get there takes. You've got to be able to enjoy the *getting there*. Don't be so tunnel-vision focused on where you're going that you forget to enjoy where you are.

So the message for tonight is: Whether you're on a Scout trip or going through life, enjoy the journey.

YOUR COMFORT ZONE II

All this talk of getting out of our comfort zones might lead you to think we should *always* be challenging ourselves. But, I don't think so.

We need our comfort zones, in all parts of our life: At home we need to be surrounded by the people (and pets, perhaps) who make us feel loved and needed; we need down time to read or binge-watch or whatever guilty pleasure suits you (true confession: I still sometimes disappear to the basement in the dead of winter and replay the original, 8-bit *Legend of Zelda* on the kids' old gaming console).

And at work, we would feel pretty incompetent if we did only new things, right? The repetition and mastery of the tasks we do well are what give us the confidence and courage to try those new pursuits.

The point is that if we do *only* the things we're comfortable with, we'll never grow. And as a wise preacher once said, "God loves you just the way you are… and he loves you too much to let you stay that way."

That's why we need to get out of our comfort zones. Not to live our lives out there, just to visit on a regular basis.

There's one final component to getting out of your comfort zone, and it's one we skip over far too often: Having made the effort to grow, having reached beyond what's normal for you, having set the bar higher in some way… take some time to give yourself a little credit.

Our hurry-up, connected world offers precious little opportunity for reflection, with our phones constantly chirping and the next thing on our to-do lists beckoning all the time. But if we don't stop and reflect upon what we've accomplished, we can't learn from it, and so we might as well not have bothered.

Ask yourself: What did this trip outside my comfort zone mean for me? What did I learn? How did I grow? What would I do differently next time? And once you answer those questions, for heaven's sake, give yourself a pat on the back for a job well done. Even if it didn't turn out as you'd hoped, give yourself some credit for having had the courage to try. Find a way to treat yourself that's proportional to the accomplishment.

I admit I'm as guilty as anyone on this front: I've always been someone with a burning need to know what's around the next corner… sometimes literally. When I was in college and pledging a fraternity we would regularly get dropped off in the middle of the night somewhere in central New York State. It was very rural, and *very* dark. Whether it was leadership or compulsion I'm not sure, but I was always out ahead of the group trying to see what was over the next hill or around the next bend, hoping it would offer a clue as to where the heck we were (and possibly a pay phone so we could call the sorority sisters who would— usually—come and pick us up. I think we did walk the whole way back to campus one time.).

There's nothing wrong with looking forward, and we'd be fools not to, but we can learn an awful lot by looking back.

Like you (I'm betting), we have a cabinet in our kitchen with far too many coffee mugs in it, more than the two of us could ever use. But out of all those mugs, I generally use four: Two are identical and bear the logo of the business peer group I joined almost immediately upon becoming an entrepreneur—one of my first and best decisions, and one you'll hear more about later. I alternate those two cups on weekdays.

The other two are from scout reservations where Troop 328 spent its summer camp week in different years (as a bonus, one says, "Thank You for Being a Camp Leader!" on it in great, big letters). My Saturday and Sunday mornings always begin with one of these.

Here's the point: Almost every single day, among my very first conscious acts is to reach out and grab a visible, tangible reminder of a time when I stepped out of my comfort zone… and of the difference it made in my life.

Scoutmaster Minute
THE SOLOIST AND THE GROUP

Author's Note: at the time this was first delivered, "American Idol" was still pretty much the only game in talent-show town. It was before "The Voice," "America's Got Talent," "Dancing with the Marginally Famous" and so forth.

How many of you watch "American Idol"? Even if you don't, I'm sure you know that the idea is to find America's next great pop star, and so thousands of people show up to audition.

What many of them have in common is that it seems their parents have spent every waking moment telling them that they're the most wonderful, special, talented thing ever to walk God's green earth... in other words, many of them are extremely self-centered and egotistical.

So it's really interesting to watch the one week each year when they take these ego cases and make them work in a group. They're put in groups of four, and they have to learn a song and come up with some choreography, and some don't handle it very well.

I've done enough singing in groups—everything from two people to choirs of 100—to know that, especially in a smaller group, it's a lot less about how well you sing and a lot more about how well you *listen*. You have to be sensitive to what's going on around you, and you have to set aside your desire to be the star, to have the spotlight, and let the people around you shine. The groups that figure that out on "Idol" do well, and the groups that don't… well, they have these awful train wrecks in front of the judges, and then they cry and have catfights and call each other bad names that get bleeped out, and it's all fun to watch.

So what does any of this have to do with Scouts? Well, there's a leadership lesson buried in here, because a good leader has to do the same things: He has to listen to the people around him, and sometimes he has to set aside his own desires for the good of the group.

One of the better definitions of a good leader is that he makes the people around him better, and he knows that if he does that he doesn't have to worry about himself.

THE SOLOIST, THE
CONDUCTOR AND THE TEAM

I s it safe to say that great leaders know how to make the people around them shine? I think it is.

I've already mentioned that I'm a singer, and that can mean as many different things as there are types of music. But for our purposes, consider the distinction between the soloist and the choir member.

The soloist is in the spotlight by choice and (again depending on the type of music) has anywhere from a little to a lot of leeway in interpreting the music in a way that he or she feels will be meaningful to an audience. Think of your own favorite singers, or for example Van Morrison's inspired riffing at the end of "Moondance"; the way Sinatra phrased his songs (pay attention to where he breathes, and more importantly, where he doesn't); the almost-whispered start to Whitney Houston's "I Will Always Love You" in contrast to the power the song achieves at its climax. These are all soloists making very individual choices, to great effect.

Now consider the choir member. He or she may still be a great singer, but any musical decisions are entirely at the direction of the conductor who interprets the music for the group, deciding where they'll breathe, how loud or soft or fast or slow the piece will go, and dozens of other details. The chorister is but a cog in the musical machine.

If musical metaphors aren't your thing, try this: The running back on a football team is often the star player. He has a general assignment on each play, but has to also react to what actually happens and often must improvise and change direction on the fly. The offensive lineman, on the other hand, toils in near-anonymity. He has a blocking assignment, and he and the rest of his linemates work in concert to make the play happen… with usually much less improvising.

As a singer I'm a bit of an odd duck in being a soloist who also loves choral singing, because just as different exercises work different muscles, solo work and choral work require different skill sets. The choral singer reins in his individuality for the betterment of the group, and the good ones quickly learn that listening to what's going on around them is every bit as important as singing accurately. The more each singer hears and understands the other parts of the choir, the better the group will be, no exceptions.

A choral singer knows that after his voice and his ears, his most important tool is the pencil he uses to notate the music, marking in the conductor's instructions on where to breathe and anything else having to do with the interpretation of the music. The *really* involved singer marks not only his own part but all the others, because that helps him better understand the piece as a whole.

There is glory and often great ego gratification in being in the spotlight as the soloist or the running back. But there is incredible satisfaction as well in being a part of a high-performing group and knowing that the way you handled your own responsibilities helped to make it that way. Some of the most challenging and satisfying work I've done as a singer has been in small, 12- to 16-voice groups singing *a cappella* music (no accompaniment... just the singers). There's nowhere to hide, and you'd better get your part right. When you do, the result can be glorious, and there's no feeling like it. Just as the offensive line celebrates a touchdown by the running back, the desired outcome is the result of everyone on the team executing their assignments near-flawlessly.

Finally, consider the conductor. I've heard people with non-musical backgrounds ask, "Why does the orchestra/choir need a conductor? They're all musicians. Don't they know how to play/sing the music on the page?" Well, yes and no. The conductor may appear to be just waving his or her arms at the group, but the act of keeping everyone together in the performance is the proverbial tip of the iceberg, the culmination of so much more unseen work in rehearsal.

In most cases, the conductor chooses the music, interprets and teaches it and is completely responsible for the outcome. How fast or how slow a certain section will go, the balance between different instrumental or vocal parts, the emotional interpretation of the piece... all this happens at the hands of the conductor.

One of the central challenges in the conductor's world is that the instructions, so to speak, are on the page in front of the musicians. But the piece really comes to life when the musicians can get their eyes up, away from the page and onto the conductor. "Get your noses out of the book!" is a frequent admonition in choir rehearsal, and musicians work hard to look down at the next section of music before it happens, and then look up and interact with the conductor while actually singing it. If you've ever heard a musical group where the players or singers weren't together, it's probably because they had their heads down.

And by the way, that's a two-way street: I occasionally have the privilege to guest-conduct our very talented choir at church, and I know from experience that if they're looking up as good singers do, but I'm looking down at *my* music, that's an opportunity wasted. The magic happens when we're making eye contact and feeding off one another's energy… that's when we really make a joyful noise.

(Pro tip: Conducting a group is also a great way to fool your smart watch into thinking you're walking a long, long way.)

So as a leader, are you the soloist, the conductor or the choral singer? Yes.

There are times when you're the one out front in the spotlight, perhaps as a speaker or presenter. You interpret the available content in a way that will be meaningful and moving to your audience (if all goes well!).

Every leader is well familiar with the role of conductor: teaching, interpreting, motivating and getting the team to work in concert. And yes, sometimes it will take some effort to get their noses out of the book—or phone or computer screen—and actually interact with you, their teammates and clients. And remember, when they do look up, you need to be there looking back.

But some of your best work as a leader will happen when you assume that role as another cog in the machine and listen—really listen—to the other parts around you, understand what they're doing and reflect upon how your own role interacts with and supports them. The more you pay attention to how in tune you are with those who surround you, the more they'll return the favor, and that makes the whole group better.

And just like the choral singer with the pencil, the better your comprehension of what all the other parts of your business are doing, the greater your understanding of the whole… and the more effective you'll be as a leader.

Scoutmaster Minute
WE ARE WHAT WE REPEATEDLY DO

I was reading recently about George Washington, whom we remember as being a man of great character—a very moral man, a great leader—and he was… but what I didn't know was that leadership didn't come naturally to him.

Washington was a student of history. He studied those who came before him, and then he would try to make himself act the way they would have acted by developing the small habits that would lead him in that direction.

Now, there are two schools of thought on that. One observer might say, "It was all an act… Washington was a phony, not this great natural leader." But the other school of thought says, "You miss the point. One of the truly great things about George Washington was that he understood that character can be *developed*. He believed that we *are what we repeatedly do*, and he worked hard to change his habits and to make himself into the great man we remember."

Habits are tricky things. We spoke about New Year's resolutions recently, and maybe some of the adults in your life are trying to eat less, exercise more and so forth. That's because habits are hard to break... but the good news is that *good* habits are hard to break, also.

I'm telling you this tonight not because it's January and I think you need to make New Years' resolutions. I'm telling you because you guys are 12, 13, 14, 15, 16 years old... and this is the stretch of your life where you develop the habits that, for better or worse, will be with you the rest of the way: your work habits, the way you eat, the way you exercise, the way you treat other people, the way you react when things don't go well.

In all of these ways and many others, you are building the foundation for the man you're going to be, and I think it's a very exciting thought that George Washington gives us: By having a goal in mind, and by practicing the habits that will lead you in that direction, you can be whomever you want to be.

LEARNING TO LEAD

In taking on the Scoutmaster role, I knew I had to teach myself to be the leader the troop needed at a very difficult time. Don't think for a minute that the effort was an unbroken string of successes. I could have used a lot more patience, for one, and the boys were too often on the receiving end of my "Scoutmaster voice" as they were loudly reprimanded for one transgression or another.

But I hope those moments were the exception and not the rule. Especially in the early days, I summoned all the compassion I had to meet the unprecedented circumstances and the deep wounds we had collectively suffered.

I've never been a fan of that phrase, "fake it 'til you make it," but in truth that's what I had to do, and there were times when it all clicked, beginning with the moment when I stepped into the circle at that first meeting and summoned those words.

I found out some years later that our Senior Patrol Leader, Ryan, who opened the circle to me that night, had some inside knowledge about who the next Scoutmaster would be, courtesy of his father, Lee, who would serve as an Assistant Scoutmaster. Ryan, now a major-market television anchor and reporter, recalled that moment during a podcast interview:

> Since we had just lost our Scoutmaster, we had to have a new one, and Scoutmaster Jim was our guy... he was kind of like the Scoutmaster in waiting. My dad was telling me, "Hey, we're going to have a transitional team; like, all the Scoutmasters will help him and be kinda like the co-Scoutmaster until he's ready to take over himself. And the minute he walked in he *was* the Scoutmaster. I mean, this guy truly is a hero. The way he was so nice to all the kids, like, just being there for us, but also just having that firm leadership presence... 'cause he cried with us, but he also showed the strength we needed.

It seems I was the last one to get the word about the whole "Scoutmaster in waiting" thing. And I certainly was no hero, maybe just the right person in the right place at a very wrong time.

The noteworthy thing there is Ryan equating both a "firm leadership presence" and "he cried with us" with good leadership. There's a great misconception that a leader should distance himself or herself from emotional involvement; that if we get down there wallowing around in our feelings among those we lead, we are somehow less effective.

I disagree. I felt the loss of the Brownings keenly, and to pretend otherwise in some misguided effort to appear more like a leader would have been dishonesty of the highest order. I didn't have to manufacture any tears, but I felt no need to hide them either. Feeling what your team is feeling and letting them know it is called empathy, and every leader needs it.

(Full disclosure: Shedding tears in public apparently was not a huge stretch for me. By the end of my time as Scoutmaster, Troop 328 may or may not have had a saying that went, "It's not an Eagle Scout ceremony until Mr. Rafferty cries." I can't confirm or deny that.)

But while empathy, or "emotional intelligence" in modern management-speak, is essential to leaders of all stripes, I don't think we can lead effectively from a place of emotion. A leader needs to be the one who doesn't get hysterical when everything is going south, the one who doesn't explode at every mistake. There is great value in maintaining an even keel.

The key is in recognizing that a calm, "firm leadership presence" doesn't translate to being a robot who hands down decisions from above. Yes, you have to make those decisions, but if you really want to be considered a leader you also need to celebrate your team's triumphs and feel their pain.

Scoutmaster Minute
THE POWER OF THE APOLOGY

How do you react… when you're wrong? When Mom or Dad calls you on something, and you know it was your fault? A lot of times we get angry or defensive, or we deny that we did anything wrong. At least that's been my experience with teenage boys… and some adults.

I read a book over the summer that had a really interesting bit of information in it: when we give a sincere apology, really look someone in the eye and say, "I'm sorry. I was wrong," there's an actual physiological change that happens in the other person. They become less angry and more inclined to want to forgive us. Pretty cool.

You guys have heard of the Toro company; they make lawnmowers and other power equipment, and when you're in that business, people sometimes hurt themselves using your products. The usual company response when that happens is to line up a bunch of lawyers and make it as difficult and expensive as possible for an injured person to sue you.

In the early 1990s Toro decided to try a different approach. Whenever someone was injured using one of their products, they sent a company representative to that person, no matter where they were. That representative would meet the person face to face and say, "We're sorry this happened." Not "It was our fault," just "We're sorry it happened, and we want to try to make sure it doesn't happen again to someone else." Over the first eight years, that simple gesture saved the Toro company some $75 million in legal costs.

So next time Mom or Dad calls you out on something you did, try looking them in the eye and saying, "I'm sorry." You might be surprised at what happens.

LEADERSHIP MEANS HAVING
TO SAY YOU'RE SORRY

There are profound business lessons in that Toro story, and yet so often we dig in our heels and refuse to admit we've done wrong, or even to acknowledge that something bad has happened to the other party. We fear losing face, we fear the liability exposure to our business, and so we choose *being* right over *doing* right.

On a Sunday evening about midway through my tenure as Scoutmaster, I received a phone call from the mother of one of my scouts. In my experience, phone calls at off hours like that are never for the purpose of sharing good news, and in this case I was right.

To set the stage just a bit: In the hierarchy of Boy Scouts, there are councils responsible for large areas (in our case, Baltimore). Those councils are subdivided into districts, so each troop belongs to a certain district within the larger council. And before I go any further, let me say that the people who work at the district level are volunteers who give countless hours of their time, and decades of their scouting experience, for the betterment of all the troops and scouting in general. They're good folks, if often a bit more gung-ho than we were as a troop.

Back to the Sunday night phone call: This woman's son, then about 15, was one of two scouts from our troop who had just returned from a weekend of leadership training put on by our district, held at a scout camp about an hour away. It was a pretty intensive 3½ day session of camping and skills training, designed for scouts with some experience already under their belts.

October in our part of the world brings some unpredictable weather, and the young men who'd signed up for this event in this particular year had endured sideways rain and temperatures in the mid 40s from the time they arrived after school on Thursday until their return on Sunday evening. It's a challenge for even the most focused and experienced tent campers to keep dry under those conditions, and needless to say, even the best group of 15- and 16-year-olds is neither that focused nor that experienced.

So they slept in wet sleeping bags, shivered their way through the weekend in sodden clothes and came home exhibiting red hands, feet and faces... classic exposure symptoms. It was nothing life-threatening, but try telling a mom that when her little man comes home looking like the "before" picture in a hand lotion ad. And this particular mom was a nurse, so she was not exaggerating his condition. The other boy from our troop who'd attended had had a similar experience, and both families were pretty hot about it.

A little investigating revealed that the district leaders who'd organized the event had made exactly zero concessions to the nasty weather: The program wasn't shortened, nothing was moved indoors, *nada*. The show went on as planned, weather be damned.

There are two schools of thought here regarding the scouting experience: one is the "what doesn't kill you makes you stronger" approach, for which we could always count on the district leadership. No inclement weather, no mishap of any kind would ever induce them to shorten or otherwise modify a planned program because in their view, that discomfort was part of the character-building quality of being a Boy Scout. Fair enough; that's a completely valid approach.

In our troop we tended a little more toward leniency, or in our view, common sense. We recognized that as a scout troop we were competing with sports and other extracurricular activities for the very limited spare time of a teenager in the 21st century, and even more importantly, for their hearts and minds. We wanted them to have experiences that would keep them coming back, not to endure weekends of misery. Don't misunderstand; we got wet and/or cold plenty of times, but we also adapted to what was happening and shortened or canceled our outings as we felt was prudent.

I already knew from personal experience the district leadership's penchant for sticking to the plan: On the adult leadership training weekend I had attended about two years before, a three-day program remarkably similar to the one held for the boys, another attendee had been found deceased in his tent on Sunday morning. Did they cancel or shorten the day's activities? Don't be silly. I will never forget the surreal experience of watching the coroner's wagon back up to the poor soul's tent… while 100 feet down the hill, the rest of us were learning how to pack a backpack. Let's just say it's not the decision I would have made.

So, faced with the situation of our two boys and their irate families, we had a pretty good idea of how it would end. Nevertheless, our troop committee chair and I arranged a meeting between the district leadership and the parents, knowing there would be fireworks.

With about 10 people involved, it took a couple of months for that meeting to become a reality, and it went just as I had expected: a lot of yelling and finger-pointing from the parents, and a lot of denials and self-justification from the district leaders. It was a lot like watching a ping-pong match: Every objection from the parents was parried, justified and knocked back across the table. And when it was over, no one was happy.

What didn't happen at that meeting was infinitely more important than what did happen, and that is really the whole point here. The next morning I sent an email to the attendees from the district. I'm paraphrasing here, but the gist of it went something like this:

> *The one thing that never happened, either at this meeting or in the weeks that elapsed before it, was anyone from the District saying to these families: "We're sorry."*
>
> *Not "It was our fault," not "We should have done things differently,"; just, "We're sorry your son had a bad experience."*
>
> *I firmly believe that a simple gesture of that nature would have diffused much of the anger you faced last evening. Instead, these families got denial, defensiveness and a litany of reasons why you were right and they were wrong, and they left the meeting angrier than when they'd arrived.*

Being right and apologizing are not mutually exclusive, and as leaders we need to learn to acknowledge what others are feeling even if we firmly believe we're not at fault. We can sincerely say, "I'm sorry you feel that way," or "I'm sorry you had a bad experience," without showing weakness. Quite the contrary.

But a word of caution: if "I'm sorry you had a bad experience" is followed by three reasons why you're right and/or it wasn't your fault, you've just undone any good you might have achieved.

A willingness to apologize might not save you millions of dollars as it did with Toro, but it will absolutely make a difference in the way you're perceived as a leader by those around you.

Scoutmaster Minute
TEAM EFFORT

Yesterday morning at the Scout Sunday service upstairs [in the church above the room where we met,] I stood in front of the congregation and told them that our troop was thriving... and I wanted to talk about that a little more tonight.

At our pancake breakfast on Saturday morning [a fundraiser for the Florida trip,] I sat and spoke with [a past Scoutmaster from our troop] while we ate, and I learned something I didn't know: During his tenure as Scoutmaster, the total size of our troop was only 8 to 10 boys. That was not very long ago, and now we're more than 30. Think about that: As he was telling me that the other day, we had half the troop here serving breakfast to 140 people, while the rest were out collecting 114 bags of groceries for Scouting for Food.

I think there are three reasons that the troop is growing and thriving. One is out of our control: It's the job the Cub Scout pack does in recruiting at the elementary school, and I hear they have a very large new den this year, which is great news.

The second reason is over there (pointing to parents): We have an incredibly committed bunch of adults here. I have a friend who's running the local rec baseball program this year. He has 30 to 40 boys signed up to play in the 11-12 age group, and he can't find *three* parents to volunteer as coaches. Meanwhile, at our pancake breakfast for the Sea Base trip, we had parents back in the kitchen working at 6 am, and they don't even have a son going on the trip. We talk a lot about Scouting and how it builds your character, but you have some great examples right in your own homes, and I hope you appreciate that.

The third reason we're doing well is you: You're working hard, having fun and enjoying each other's company, and when other people see that, they naturally want to be a part of it. You are a large part of the reason for the success of the troop, and I thank you for that. When I looked back at all we were able to accomplish this weekend, I felt really, really good about where we are as a troop, and you should be proud.

DON'T GO IT ALONE

No doubt, there is a snowball effect in any organization when things go well. That Scoutmaster Minute was delivered just over a year after the tragedy we feared would destroy the troop, and instead we were full steam ahead and thriving as never before.

In hindsight, I think there are many reasons for that: First, we talked (and listened) a lot. We made no effort to ignore or gloss over the Browning tragedy, and on several Monday evenings we skipped the Scoutmaster Minute to discuss the latest legal developments as the case wound its way through the courts.

That doesn't mean that we spent our days dwelling on what had happened, though. We made a concerted effort to plan programs that were challenging and fun, organizing plenty of camping outings and other activities and generally trying to keep everyone engaged.

And the boys did more than their share. None of us, of course, had ever experienced anything like the Browning tragedy, and we feared that the memories would prove too painful, sending them away from the scouting program. But what happened was exactly the opposite. As a group, they embraced the troop and the scouting program, and in that first year they garnered merit badges and rank advancements at a clip well beyond the norm.

Finally, as with any organization, the troop thrived because everyone was on board. I mentioned earlier that many parents took on additional responsibilities, the aforementioned pancake breakfast being just one example. But without the enthusiasm of the scouts themselves and the incredible resolve and resilience they displayed in that first year, even all the adult efforts would have been meaningless.

In relating the story of that committee meeting where I was named Scoutmaster, I mentioned that three other troop dads had all volunteered to serve as Assistant Scoutmasters. I also mentioned that all three were far more qualified than I was, and that I accepted the position in part because of their promises to help.

It's easy to make pledges like those in the heat of the moment, and trust me when I say that the emotions of that particular moment were like no other. I don't think anyone would have been too surprised if Lee or Ethan or Mike (or any of the other parents who stepped up and took on new roles in the troop) had later found reasons to beg off on their commitments, in whole or in part.

Again, what actually happened was quite the opposite. All three over-delivered on the time and dedication they brought to the table, and the young men of Troop 328 found themselves in the very capable hands of a great team.

Lee, who had grown up in our neighborhood and was himself an Eagle Scout from our troop, took on the program planning, meeting with the senior scouts to lay out plans for our meetings and activities. His experience and knowledge took so much worry and work off my plate.

Ethan was also an Eagle Scout, and an outdoorsman extraordinaire. He was the go-to guy for our camping excursions, and if we were really lucky he would cook for the adults on the trip as well (I have very fond memories particularly of a chicken pot pie cooked in a Dutch oven). Really the only downside to having Ethan along on a camping outing was the virtual certainty that it would rain.

Mike was also a really well-rounded outdoorsman, though one without a scouting background. He would help with whatever needed doing at any point, and he brought to the table natural leadership skills and a wicked sense of humor that the boys loved.

For roughly the next five years, the boys of Troop 328 had not just one leader who cared and took a personal interest in them… they had four (and in fairness, many more in other positions). And just as we had envisioned, I was largely free to be the front man and the communicator, knowing that the heavy lifting would be handled and handled well. Don't misunderstand; I did my share of admin work and planning, but having those three to work with as a team made the troop so much better, especially in the early going. They were willing to be my training wheels while I learned all the ins and outs of the scouting program and how a troop really functioned.

And it all just clicked. We liked each other… and still do, gathering for a beer a couple of times a year to this day. Through all the activities and adventures, all the challenges wrought by the boys and their parents, I can't remember a single serious disagreement, just four guys all paddling in the same direction.

You might be the greatest leader since Eisenhower… and you might not. Either way, you will be a *better* leader with a team around you, and specifically a team whose skills complement your own. Many historians, in fact, credit Eisenhower more as an administrator and manager of diverse personalities (would *you* like to try managing George S. Patton?) than as a military strategist.

Our team came about through a combination of tragedy and serendipity. Lee, Ethan, Mike and I weren't chosen from a bunch of applicants, it just worked out that we were the right people in the right place at a challenging time.

Putting together your own team will require more planning, and seeking those who are good at the things that are your weaknesses. That requires a level of honesty and self-awareness that we don't always achieve. It's easy to feel threatened by the proximity of someone who's good at doing things we don't grasp so well.

But that is one mark of an effective leader: In your heart of hearts, you understand what your weaknesses are, and you know that bringing people on board to shore up those areas makes you stronger, not weaker.

And what if you're a solopreneur and don't have a team? It's even more important that you don't go it alone. Among the first things I did when I launched my consultancy was to join a business peer group. Once each month we sit around a conference room table all morning and try to solve each other's problems, asking pointed questions and giving honest, unvarnished advice.

Getting solid business and life advice from others who've been there and done that is invaluable, but I find it even more rewarding when I can help someone else solve a problem. Especially in the early days of my consulting career, it was a huge confidence booster to discover that my guidance really did have value for other businesspeople. And if that's not enough, you'll grow your network with people who really know and understand what you do. More on this later.

Look for similar opportunities where you are, and if you can't find such a group, launch one yourself. You're already meeting people at networking events, right? Round up a handful of non-competitors, starting with people you feel like you "click" with. You'll be amazed at how much you get out of it.

If you're really lucky, you'll still be getting together for a beer with your team a decade from now.

Scoutmaster Minute
THANKSGIVING

I was very fortunate to be able to spend my last semester of college in London. It was the fall semester, so I was there for Thanksgiving... except of course they don't celebrate Thanksgiving in England; it's an American holiday. Someone was on the ball, though, and they found a little inn out in the country and took us there for a traditional Thanksgiving dinner... turkey, stuffing, mashed potatoes, the whole deal. It was a wonderful touch of home for kids who'd been away for three months, and I think it was my most memorable Thanksgiving.

(As an aside, the inn had a barn which was built from the timbers of the Mayflower... a very cool piece of history, and again, very appropriate for Thanksgiving.)

So here we are (mumble) years later, and Thanksgiving 2008 is upon us. This year, it seems that we have less to be thankful for... we've had a very difficult year as a Troop, and the news and the economy have just been terrible. I imagine you've noticed that your parents are concerned about it, and everyone is just generally in a cranky mood.

So we have to work a little harder at being thankful, and go back to the basics. For instance, as far as I know, everybody in this room is in generally good health. We all have a nice, warm home to go back to, a bed to sleep in, enough to eat and a family who loves us. You don't have to go very far to find people who can't take those things for granted.

And here's the thing about being thankful: If you make a habit of it, it can make you feel better about things. When you give thanks you're focusing on what's *right* instead of what's wrong; focusing on what you *have* instead of what you don't have, because there's *always* stuff you don't have.

So by all means, this Thursday take a few moments to give thanks as you should. But I hope you'll take a moment every day to give thanks... we have a lot to be grateful for. Have a wonderful Thanksgiving.

GRATITUDE

G ratitude was a recurring theme in my talks with the scouts over those years, and it continues to be a focus for me each and every day.

In a moment you'll encounter another Scoutmaster Minute called "The Wind at Your Back," which also addresses the need to make gratitude a habit. It's worth noting that I first shared it with the scouts in early 2009, long before we descended into our current environment of name-calling and social-media shaming, especially as relates to politics. Put another way, what was once a steady trickle of negativity in the media we consume has become a fire hose. I believe the message of gratitude is even more important today, and that we need to work harder than ever to overcome the chorus of voices shouting about everything that's wrong in our world.

In my early days of entrepreneurship there were some lean times, as with any new venture, and I felt the need to put some extra effort into staying positive. I started doing an end-of-day mental exercise I had read about, and I continue to this day: The last thing I do before I close my eyes at night is to come up with three things that happened that day for which I'm grateful.

Then and now, there are days when it's very hard to come with three things ("Well, my wife still loves me..."). But there are also days where it's a challenge to choose *which* three things were the best out of all the good things that happened that day. And that in itself is a wonderful exercise in prioritizing and understanding the things that are really most important. Even on the most challenging of days there's much to be thankful for. It takes effort and discipline to remind ourselves of that, but it's effort well spent because it gets us past the wasted energy spent dwelling on what's wrong.

The problem is the alternative: As I pointed out to the scouts, it's very easy for complaining to become a habit. At the home improvement company, we had an employee, a lady of a certain age, who was a lovely person. It was often her job, however, to field the phone calls from grumpy customers. When you're remodeling people's homes, things happen... fixtures are delayed, emergencies require personnel to be taken off a project for a time, schedules run over, projects are delayed. In some way or another, things often do not go according to plan. And when those things happened, she usually took the call and did her best to straighten things out, and she was good at that.

The other thing that would happen after one of those cranky phone calls was this: Every single employee who walked in the door for the rest of the day would hear about that call in all its glorious detail. Again and again she would relive the moment, perpetuating the cycle of misery for herself and everyone within earshot (including yours truly).

A Facebook acquaintance devotes probably two-thirds of his posts to complaining, mostly about all the idiots out there on the road. Believe me, I have more than my share of issues with other drivers, but sharing them just feels like living through each negative thing a second time. Again, it's an easy thing to do, and one that becomes a habit that's hard to break.

I choose instead to make a habit of gratitude, so just as my day begins with one of those coffee mugs as a reminder of good things that have happened, it ends with a positive thought. Am I happy all the time? Of course not. Trust me, I have enough pet peeves to start my own shelter. But the daily discipline of seeking out the good helps to do for the attitude what the daily discipline of getting on a treadmill can do for the body.

Scoutmaster Minute
THE WIND AT YOUR BACK

I went out for a run yesterday afternoon. It was pretty cold and gray, and when I turned the corner onto the main road there was about a 25 mile-per-hour wind in my face (and when you're old and slow like me, that's the last thing you need). I thought, "Well, that's okay because on the way back I'll feel that wind helping me along."

I realized much later in the day that on the way back I hadn't noticed the wind at all. It was still windy out, but I hadn't noticed it on my return trip because it was blowing in the same direction I was moving.

I think that's how we are as we go through our days... we tend to notice the things we don't like, but not necessarily all the things that are good. When we turn on the shower and hot water comes out, we don't give it a second thought, but if the water's cold, we sure notice.

I'm not suggesting that you kneel down and say a prayer of thanks every time you flip a switch and the light comes on, but if we notice only the bad things, it gets to be a habit, and we fall into a routine of doing nothing but whining and complaining.

So here's my suggestion: I know you're busy with school and sports and Scouts, but try to find those moments every day when the good things happen.

Focus on the things that are good, and enjoy it when the wind is at your back.

HOLD THEIR ATTENTION

I've already given myself a bit of a pat on the back for being able to hold the attention of a group of young men who were diverse in age, background and interests, and some of whom had trouble with their attention spans in the best of circumstances. But I might just do it again here.

Toward the end of my tenure as Scoutmaster I was busy trying to get my new business up and running, and a Monday evening meeting rolled around before I had time to prepare a new Scoutmaster Minute. So I dug into my archives and found one from my very early days, about four years earlier. I was up front with the boys about this; it was April, and I remember joking that in honor of Earth Day I was going to recycle a Scoutmaster Minute (it was the one you just read about the wind at your back).

We circled up, I delivered the opening line, and out of the corner of my eye I saw Scott, one of our older scouts, nod to himself, smile and murmur, "I remember this one."

If you've been a parent of teenagers, tell me this: When was the last time your child remembered anything you said four years later?

Or 10 minutes?

So what were the keys to being memorable, and how can you duplicate them in your next speech, staff meeting or sales presentation? Here's what I think.

First, I had perhaps an unfair advantage or two in that I was speaking to a group that already knew and trusted me, and who were motivated to be there. Those qualifiers may not apply to the blank faces around the conference table the next time you deliver an important presentation to co-workers or sales prospects. Nevertheless, I approached each Scoutmaster Minute as a mini-presentation. No matter how well we all knew and cared for each other, it was still on me to hold the boys' attention, and so it is on you.

With apologies to the Boy Scouts, Step One is pretty obvious: Be prepared. You need to know your material cold so that when the unexpected happens—and it will—you're not thrown off your message.

My routine generally went like this: I would get an idea for the next Scoutmaster Minute and then spend the next few days speaking it out loud in my car as I commuted to and from the office. The act of actually speaking the words is vital; just writing down your thoughts or memorizing bullet points will not give you a feel for the rhythm of what you're presenting.

The repetition here is really important, too. As you get familiar with your material, you'll find yourself rearranging the sequence, dropping some things that you initially thought were important and generally trimming away the fat. You'll wind up with a lean message that's much more likely to hold the attention of the group.

Note, however, that practicing and polishing does not mean memorizing word for word. It's going to be a little different every time, and so it should. You're not in a contest to recite the Gettysburg

Address; you're trying to win people over to your point of view—whether they're staff, bosses or potential clients. And you do that by speaking *to* them as you would with friends, not by reciting memorized boilerplate *at* them.

DON'T READ TO THEM. For the love of God, don't read to them. I have been a professional radio announcer and voice-over artist for more than half my life. I can take a written script and make it sound as personal and conversational as you'd like, and that takes years of practice that you probably haven't had. And even though I *can* do that, I never did read anything off the page to the scouts, with two exceptions: statistics and quotations.

I am willing to bet that you've sat through a session where the presenter felt compelled to read Every. Word. On. Every. Slide. And I am also willing to bet that at that moment you wished you were having a colonoscopy instead. Don't be that guy or gal.

Now, if your slide has three bullet points on it and you really feel like the second one is vital information, feel free to say, "Be sure to note the middle bullet there, which shows that XYZ company saw a 23% increase in customer satisfaction after deploying our software…" That's fair game for sure, but your job as a presenter is to bring the slides to life in a meaningful way, not to parrot them word for word.

Tell stories. This is not news to anyone, and I have followed the standard business-book formula here of opening the chapter with a story to illustrate the point. For some reason, though, our logical brains always think our audience will be wowed or motivated by the unassailable logic of facts and figures. They will, but only if those facts and figures grow from a compelling story. For a really great and much deeper dive into this, I highly recommend "Conversations that Win the Complex Sale" by Erik Peterson and Tim Riesterer.[2]

---

2   Erik Peterson and Tim Riesterer, Conversations that Win the Complex Sale (McGraw-Hill Education, 2011).

Have a Plan B. Golfers like to talk about having a bail-out area. We all hope that every shot will go where we intend (despite years of evidence to the contrary), but we still might approach a certain green thinking, "I want to miss left here if I'm going to miss. On the right, there are three bunkers, a water hazard and... say, is that an alligator sunning himself on the bank?"

Your bail-out area will hopefully not involve large reptiles, but you need to be prepared for that moment 10 minutes into your scheduled 45-minute presentation when the client's phone buzzes and she says, "I'm sorry, but I'm going to have to cut this short. I can give you another 10 minutes." Be ready to skip to the parts you've already decided were most vital. Because you prepared.

Even if your client isn't cutting you short, you need to read the room. Though you're doing most of the talking, communication is flowing in both directions, and if your audience is crossing and uncrossing their legs, checking their phones, looking at the door, etc., you'll be happy you were ready with the Spark Notes version of your pitch.

An extreme example: In my years as a home improvement marketer I entertained an endless parade of salespeople from every TV and radio station, newspaper, magazine, Yellow Pages (dating myself a bit again), you name it. One day I met with a young lady from a local magazine who sat down across the table from me and propped up her presentation book to lead me by the hand through their demographics, circulation figures and so forth. And then it got a little silly:

HER: And we also sponsor this event (a weekly summer concert series at a local retail complex).

ME: Oh, I know. We've been to it a few times to see a band we like. It's a lot of fun. You guys have your branding on the camp chairs they lend out.

HER (flips page): They have a band there every week.

ME: Yes, I know. We've been there several times.

HER   (flips page): And our magazine supplies the camp chairs.

ME: Yes, I know. We've been there several times.

HER   (flips page): It's an event that draws a lot of people, and we're very visible there.

ME: Yes, I know. Could we maybe skip to the next thing?

HER   (flips page): So we get a lot of visibility at this event, and there's a band. And we sponsor the chairs.

ME: <bangs head on table>

There is very little exaggeration in that story. She really was that tone-deaf to what was happening around her, and even after I asked her directly to move on to the next section she clung to that pitch book like it was the last life preserver on the *Titanic*.

Don't be that gal or guy either.

You've probably gathered by now that I have a sense of humor, and that was a central part of my interactions with the scouts all the time, not just when I was speaking to the group. If you're good at making people laugh, by all means make that a part of your interactions. And if humor doesn't come naturally to you, that's okay too. The best thing you can do in front of any group is to be yourself.

That does not, however, mean you should lead off with the joke about the one-armed pirate to "warm up the room." Humor in a business setting needs to grow naturally out of the circumstances (and it's also a great arrow to have in your quiver as a manager, especially if you can direct it at yourself).

In the end it comes down to belief in yourself and your message, whether you're selling something or not. Belief in your product allows you to speak confidently about it without using the pitch book as a crutch. Belief in your preparation allows you to roll with the punches when things don't go as planned.

And belief in yourself comes with experience. As mentioned previously, I'm not a fan of that "fake it 'til you make it" saying, but the fact is that at some point you'll be doing something like this for the first time. I think—and hope—that the scouts were largely unaware of my massive misgivings about leading them, especially in that first year. I was very transparent with them over my lack of experience, but I took pains to appear confident regardless, and after a time it stopped being just an appearance and became a reality.

So if you can't believe in yourself because you *have done* something, believe for certain that you *can do* it. As Henry Ford said, "Whether you think you can or think you can't, you're right."

Scoutmaster Minute
RECALCULATING

Have you ever been in a car when the driver ignores what the GPS says to do? It says to turn right and the driver goes straight, and what happens? The GPS gets confused and it says, "Recalculating..." because now it's on a road it didn't expect to be on and it has to figure out a new way to get you to your destination.

You are going to have some moments in your life, if you haven't already, when you find yourself on a road you didn't expect to be traveling. These tend to be life's challenging moments: Something you were hoping for didn't happen, or something unexpected did happen... maybe you don't get into the college you're hoping for, or don't get to date the girl you have a thing for. When you get older it gets even more serious: A relationship doesn't work out, or a job, or even a career. The really hard part is to understand that these moments don't mean you're lost... like the GPS, you have to *recalculate* and find another to get where you want to go.

I've been fired twice in my life (both times back when I was in the radio business), and they were not happy moments in either case. I can look back today and understand that if both of those events hadn't happened I wouldn't be here tonight, or even living in Maryland, and I wouldn't change a thing... but I'll tell you very honestly that I got here via a very different route than the one I programmed into my personal GPS way back when. It involved a good deal of *recalculating*. I am walking proof of the line that goes something like, "Life is what happens to you while you're making other plans."

When you hit those roadblocks and detours in your life, I think the key is having the faith to believe that things work out for the best, even if they don't go as you planned. Be willing to *recalculate*... you might find the road you wind up on is even better than the one you planned.

THE ROADS NOT TAKEN

Well, make that *three* times…

I remember delivering that line about having been fired twice, and that it elicited a little gasp from the scouts. Flush with the confidence of youth as they were, I guess it hadn't occurred to them that one of their adult leaders would have had any life setbacks like that. My goal wasn't to shock or rattle them but to plant the idea that opportunities often disguise themselves as failure.

I've endured more than my share of "recalculating" over my lifetime, and I have somewhat mixed feelings about it all. I'm sure there were periods when I was too complacent, too willing to just allow things to happen instead of *making* them happen. Yet when I look at the whole picture, there's very little I would want to change.

Perhaps you've had this experience: You go to your high school reunion and run into the couple who dated each other back when you were all in school together. Now they're married, and both are working in the careers they chose way back then to boot. It's as if they had made a list when they were 16, and then just checked off the boxes as they went: career, *check*. Marriage, *check*. 2.2 kids, *check*... no deviations, no detours, no *recalculating*, just everything in perfect, linear order.

In certain ways I've always envied those folks whose lives seem to be an unbroken straight line... how nice it must be to never miss a turn on the road of life, and to always know what's ahead. In other ways, though, I wonder what they've missed. I've wound up in so many great places, many of which were never part of the plan, including all the outdoor adventures described herein.

Of course, I didn't *have* much of a plan, at least not at 16. I was a pretty good musician as a high-schooler, but I sensed that I didn't have the chops (or the discipline) to pursue music performance as a career, and I didn't want to be a music teacher. So I thought, "Radio & TV Communications sounds like fun," and off I went. And it worked out okay, until it didn't. I rose to the level of full-time announcer, and then Program Director, in major markets like Philadelphia and Baltimore, then found myself out of work during a recession... and I *recalculated*.

We can eat ourselves alive wondering what might have been. As I began my senior year of college, I had to decide between a full-time internship at a TV station and one at a radio station. I chose radio, and I've always wondered where the other path would have led. More money? Probably. Greater fame? Maybe. More stress? Undoubtedly. But most significantly, I likely would never have met my amazing wife, Monica, because we first bumped into each other in the Philadelphia suburb where I worked for a radio station. That in itself is enough to make me stop with the "what ifs."

Recent years have brought a new and dangerous dimension to this self-evaluation we like to do, because now everyone else's life is on full display for us on social media. It's hard not to compare notes, to ponder what we don't have, to think about what might have been if we had just done this or that differently.

In 2018, the Philadelphia Eagles won the Super Bowl behind backup quarterback Nick Foles. In this case, the term "backup quarterback" doesn't really tell the story. Try "backup journeyman quarterback who had bounced around the league and had already contemplated retirement at age 26." It was a stunning performance throughout the playoffs and in defeating the heavily favored New England Patriots in the championship game. But for me, what followed was even more special.

In a press conference less than an hour after the game, still in sweats, Foles delivered one of the most remarkable off-the-cuff statements I've ever heard. A reporter asked what Foles wanted fans to take away from his journey (talk about recalculating!) and he responded:

> I think the big thing is don't be afraid to fail. In our society today—you know, Instagram, Twitter, it's a highlight reel. It's all the good things. And then when you look at it, you think, like, wow, when you have a rough day or your life's not as good as that, you're failing.
>
> "Failure is a part of life. That's a part of building character and growing. Like, without failure, who would you be? I wouldn't be up here if I hadn't fallen thousands of times, made mistakes. We all are human. We all have weaknesses."[3]

"It's a highlight reel." Truer words were never spoken.

The next time you start to feel a little envious of the life someone else is living, as you view their vacation photos from Cabo or their new car or their self-congratulatory LinkedIn post, remember that there's far more behind the curtain, for all of us. Few of us take to Twitter or Instagram to share our secret doubts, our struggles with depression or

---

3   Nick Foles, 2018, reported by Business Insider.

addiction, the heartache our kids are capable of delivering, our marital difficulties… the list goes on. Don't be fooled into thinking you're less than you are because you're comparing yourself to the funhouse mirror reflection of someone else's life online.

Recalculating is not failure. Having a less shiny life than your Facebook friends is not failure. Failure is only failure if you don't get up and try again. Speaking of which…

Scoutmaster Minute
GETTING UP AGAIN

A few weeks ago the PGA Tour (professional golfers) wrapped up its season in Orlando. On the last day, a guy named D.J. Gregory walked up the 18th hole with the rest of the crowd… and completed his goal of walking every hole on every course on every round of the PGA Tour in 2008, a total of 3,256 golf holes.

Why is that a big deal? D.J. Gregory was born with Cerebral Palsy. Doctors told his parents he would probably never walk at all, and he had five surgeries on his legs by the time he reached first grade. He not only learned to walk, he managed to get both a Bachelor's and Masters' degree in Sports Management before he got this idea.

On his quest this year from March through November, D.J. walked nearly 1,000 miles on the golf course. That's impressive enough, but think about all the getting from place to place, going through airports and so on. He traveled nearly 80,000 miles, covering 23 states and three countries. He also drank about 300 bottles each of water, sports drinks and soda.

One more statistic, which D.J. himself kept: He fell down 29 times. He also got up 29 times.[4]

---

4   Reported by ABC News, November 14, 2008.

Scoutmaster Minute
OPPORTUNITY DISGUISED AS FAILURE

Guys, I hope you have a handkerchief handy, because tonight we're going to talk about Oprah...

You probably know that before she was really famous, Oprah was a TV host here in Baltimore. What I didn't know was that she was a news anchor, and she was demoted to hosting a daytime talk show. When they brought her in to tell her, she was not happy about it... she cried, and said, "Don't do this to me. Daytime television is the lowest of the low." (She may have been right about that last part).

Anyway, she did host the show, then she moved on to Chicago and hosted a similar show that was syndicated into the one that made her a billionaire with a 'b'... so you'd have to say that that little bit of career disappointment in Baltimore turned out ok for her.

And that's the point tonight: As you go through life you're going to find that sometimes opportunity disguises itself as failure. You guys are all very bright and very successful at what you do, and I hate to break it to you, but at some point you're going to fail at something: You won't make the team or make the first string, you musicians will audition unsuccessfully for something, you won't get into the college of your choice or get to date the girl you like. And when that happens, the disappointment can be intense. We get our hearts set on something, and when it doesn't happen it's very hard to deal with.

What you'll find is that after some time passes, in many cases you'll be able to look back and realize that what happened worked out for the best. I'm old enough to be able to be grateful for some of the jobs I interviewed for and didn't get, and yes, even some of the girls who declined to go out with me (hard to imagine, I know).

We watched a movie recently that had a wonderful line delivered by an actor playing a priest: "God always answers our prayers, but the answer is not always the one we wanted."[5]

---

5   Angels and Demons, 2009, Director Ron Howard, Sony Pictures

JOB I WAS BETTER THAN

O pportunity truly is a master of disguise. Sometimes, as we just discussed, it looks a whole lot like failure. But it takes other forms as well.

Let's circle back for a moment to two things from that last chapter: First, sometimes I was too complacent, no doubt. And second, the "finding myself out of work during a recession" part.

In 1989 I moved to Baltimore to take a position as Program Director of an FM radio station. A management reshuffle at my previous gig (as an Assistant Program Director in Philadelphia) had left me out of the game of musical chairs, and a few months later the Baltimore opportunity arose.

It looked like a promising one, too: a pretty good company, great penthouse offices and a music format I had a lot of experience with. So I loaded up the car in February and headed south, and as I hit the first main road "New Kid in Town" by the Eagles came on the radio. Clearly it was meant to be. (As a bonus, Monica and I were to be married later that year. Moving to Baltimore got me out of much of the wedding planning. Winning!)

What I didn't understand was the history of the station: Over the previous decade, they had tried about 10 different formats, all under the same name, with the result that the general public really didn't have any idea of what the station was. People knew where to go for easy listening, or for rock and roll, but 92 STAR didn't really hold a specific position in anyone's mind, and so Attempt Number 11 didn't go so well.

Almost exactly two years later, they decided to change formats again, and now we come to that "out of work during a recession" juncture. To be honest, I probably would have done the same thing if I had been in charge there, and to this day I'm friendly with the boss who fired me, now the general manager of a TV station.

But still, I was out of work. And not much hiring was going on.

Determined to stay somewhere in the mid-Atlantic region, I started firing off resumes (via typewriter and fax machine... the struggle was real). And then I buried a few copies in the yard, with pretty much the same result. Months slogged by, and while I used some of the time productively by quitting smoking and starting to run myself into shape, by the time summer rolled around I was getting a little stir crazy.

An acquaintance from my volleyball league was the VP of a local remodeling company and needed an extra set of hands. Having time and needing money, I agreed, and reported for duty very early one morning to a large apartment complex in Baltimore to begin my career as a roofer's helper.

There are not too many spots on the home-improvement food chain lower than that occupied by the roofer's helper: We were installing shingled roofs on large apartment buildings in August. This involved many fun tasks, including carrying 80-pound bundles of shingles up a

40-foot ladder. We worked from 6 am to about 2 pm because after that, the shingles would melt under your shoes.

I remember coming home after the first day of work and Monica asking me how my day had been. I said, "There are two kinds of jobs: Those where you shower before work, and those where you shower after work. This is the second kind." But I kept at it, for lack of a better offer.

When the weather started to cool, the company moved me to an indoor project, to help a carpenter who was remodeling a kitchen and bath—a big improvement in many ways. And then my friend the VP came to me and asked if I would consider working in the office instead.

Behind its offices, the company had a 3,000-square-foot warehouse where they parked trucks and kept building materials as well as cabinets and fixtures for pending projects. They were experiencing what efficiency experts call "slippage" and what construction guys call "s**t walking away." They needed someone with some organizational skills to keep an eye on things, and to their credit encouraged me to keep looking for radio work and even to use their fax machine to send resumes around if I wished.

The next full-time radio job never came, and I stayed there until the new owner showed me the door more than two decades later.

The company did a lot of advertising, and for that they retained an agency in town. In the early days the owner would show me a radio script, for example, that the agency had provided, and ask my opinion. I would have a go at rewriting it, and invariably they liked mine more. Eventually, they said goodbye to the agency, brought the advertising in-house, and I had a real job and a new title. A few years later the longtime sales manager retired and I added his responsibilities.

It's a great story, but those things happened over years, not months. Too complacent? Maybe. But a part of me is proud that: a) I didn't look down my nose at blue-collar work; and b) I stuck with it and turned it into a real career.

Which is why it resonated like a gong with me in 2013 when Ashton Kutcher accepted, of all things, a Nickelodeon Teen Choice Award. Here's an excerpt of what he said:

> I believe that opportunity looks a lot like hard work... When I was 13 I had my first job with my dad carrying shingles up to the roof. And then I got a job washing dishes at a restaurant. And then I got a job in a grocery store deli. And then I got a job in a factory sweeping Cheerio dust off the ground. And I've never had a job in my life that I was better than. I was always just lucky to have a job. And every job that I had was a stepping stone to my next job and I never quit my job until I had my next job. And so opportunities look a lot like work.[6]

I've never had a job in my life that I was better than. For a guy who'd been a roofer's helper and a warehouse manager, that hit the mark. My tenure as a scout leader was done before that speech was delivered, or there would have been a Scoutmaster minute about it the very next Monday.

And there is opportunity's other disguise: hard work.

---

6   Ashton Kutcher, 2013. Reported by genius.com.

Scoutmaster Minute
TEACHING

(To Cub/Webelos Scouts visiting that evening prior to "bridging over" to Boy Scouts): So guys, you've had a look at how our meetings go: We conduct some business, learn skills, play a game and so forth. What you might have noticed is that while your Cub Scout meetings were run by adult leaders, a lot more of the meetings here are conducted by the Scouts. The adults are here to guide you, but the boys run things as much as possible.

And there's a lesson there that will help you not only in Scouting, but in school: There are at least three ways to learn something. First, you can memorize it real fast, spit it out on your test paper the next day (or to your Scoutmaster) and forget it; second, you can take some more time and really learn it, which is better. But the best way of all to learn something... is to teach it to someone else. That's how you really *know* you know it. And that's when Scouting really works... these guys teach you the way the guys before them taught them, and in a few years you'll teach the ones who come after you.

HANDING OFF THE BALL

E very business leader struggles with delegating work. We have just enough ego (and sometimes a little left over) to believe that we're the only one who can do that voodoo that we do so well. The problem is that growth depends on our ability to focus on the bigger-picture things that make our companies better. Most of us spend far too few of our hours on the pursuits that can be considered the highest and best uses of our time, and far too many on tasks that others could handle, thus freeing us to do more of the good stuff.

So how do we get over our fear of letting go of these tasks? How do we teach them to others in a way that will make us comfortable enough to step away? The answers, I believe, lie in the ways we educate others to step in and take over.

As you know, the scouting program moves young people through a series of ranks on their way to Eagle Scout (the vast majority, of course, never get there). A young man joining the program begins without a rank (and is typically called simply a "Scout") and then moves on through the ranks of Tenderfoot, Second Class, First Class, Star, Life and finally, Eagle.

In order to achieve each rank, a scout literally has to check a series of boxes on the back pages of his Scouting Handbook indicating mastery of a variety of skills, and have each one confirmed by an adult leader. And these lists are considerable: nearly 40 tasks for the rank of First Class, for example, on top of those already completed to achieve Tenderfoot and Second Class.

Especially in the early going, these tend to be bite-sized achievements: Learn to tie a certain knot; plan, shop for and prepare a meal for several others on a camping trip; demonstrate a specific first-aid skill; attend a community meeting and explain what was debated. In other words, a really big task—achieving the next rank—is broken down into many smaller, manageable tasks.

Something else that's notable about the BSA's rank progressions: Up to the rank of First Class, the requirements are mostly about the "nuts and bolts" of scouting: outdoor skills, first aid, knot tying and so forth. From there onward, the rank requirements revolve around increased time in leadership roles and community service as the scout approaches Eagle. The requirements for Star, Life and Eagle become much fewer in number and much greater in the amount of time, responsibility, dedication and self-direction required of the scout... which is why so few make it all the way to Eagle.

So tell me: Does that sound like the beginnings of a plan to start taking some things off your own plate in the workplace? Could you delegate, say, your billing by breaking it down into smaller, manageable tasks and making sure an employee demonstrates mastery of each one before moving on to the next? And as they do that, would it make sense to give them increasing responsibility and latitude for self-direction? Of course it would.

This topic of delegation is addressed brilliantly and in great detail in a book called "Clockwork" by Mike Michalowicz. As the title might suggest, it's about getting your business to run without you… like clockwork. Obviously, a huge component of that is being able to get things off your own to-do list, and Mike does a great job of diving into what to do and what not to do. (Hint: Those big policy manuals up on the shelf? The ones no one ever touches? That's what not to do.)[7]

The scouting program, by design, addresses delegation, because the continual goal is the scout-led troop. In other words, the ideal situation is one in which the boys are planning the meetings and camping trips and generally running the program, with minimal adult intervention. That's the goal, but the reality is often somewhat different, and there are many missteps along the way (one example that jumps to mind is our patrol that planned their own meals for a weekend camping trip… and showed up with frozen pizzas, apparently unaware that there were not actually any ovens—or freezers—at the campsite).

In scouting as in business, this ability to take on tasks of increasing responsibility is what really separates the average person from the achievers, isn't it? There's no magic bullet that will make everyone in your business step up and become capable of doing everything you do, but the only way to find out who can and who can't is to let them try. So let's look at how to bring them along.

The BSA promotes the EDGE method for teaching: Explain, Demonstrate, Guide and Enable.

If you were to apply the EDGE method to, say, making a peanut butter and jelly sandwich (as they sometimes do in scout training sessions), you would:

- Explain: tell someone how you're going to take two pieces of bread, apply peanut butter to one and jelly to the other and

---

7   Mike Michalowicz, Clockwork (Portfolio, 2018).

then marry them into a sandwich. You might even mention that when you're done, the peanut butter and jelly will be on the *inside*.

- Demonstrate: actually make a PBJ with the person watching.
- Guide: have the person now make their own PBJ as you stand over their shoulder, ready to correct any missteps.
- Enable: turn them loose to make PBJs at their own discretion.

In a business setting, there's one more step that's not quite covered by the word "enable," and again this comes from "Clockwork": you must allow the person to whom you're delegating the task to take *ownership* of the outcome. To look back at our earlier example of handing off your billing, the person you're delegating the tasks to must have both the authority and the responsibility to be held accountable for your receivables, however you choose to measure that. You haven't truly delegated a task until the responsibility for its success has been handed off also.

It's a scary thing for any leader, because we all know that sooner or later one of the people who reports to you is going to do the business equivalent of bringing frozen pizza to a campsite, with probably far worse consequences.

But the upside is so much greater. Nearly every employee wants a path to increased responsibilities, and the more engaged you can keep your team, the more likely they are to stick around. Economies change, but as I write this, the main complaint I hear from business owners is, "I can't find enough good people." Let your good people do good things and they'll attract even more good people.

Happier employees, less on your own plate, and you might even get a PBJ out of the deal. Everybody wins!

Scoutmaster Minute
THE UNIFORM

Imagine this: You're in the lobby of a museum in the city, and a man you've never seen walks in the front door with his two children – both under age 5 – and says to you, "Would you mind watching my children while I go park my car?" Can you imagine your parents doing that – leaving you with a complete stranger when you were that small?

It really happened, and here's why: The people in the lobby of the museum were a Scout troop and their leaders, in uniform. Picture the situation: It was a rainy day, the dad was probably double-parked outside and had two small kids with strollers and all the other stuff, and he needed help. He saw Scout uniforms and decided immediately that these were people he could trust with his most precious possessions.

I tell you this story because I know that many of you aren't thrilled when we ask you to wear your Scout uniform in public, and I understand. But I want you to understand that your Scout shirt says a bunch of things about you, and they're all good. We could go on and on about what those things are, but the bottom line is just what the man in the museum figured out at a glance: You're someone who can be trusted, and you don't have to watch the news too long to understand that the world needs more of that.

I'm not suggesting that you wear your uniform every time you go to the mall; I just wanted to remind you that your uniform isn't something to be embarrassed about. Quite the contrary; it means you're one of the good guys.

FATHER AND SON

Well, nice try.

I can't say I was ever very successful in getting all of the young men of Troop 328 to embrace the uniform, including my own offspring. The church where we had our troop meetings is less than two blocks from our house, so we would usually walk to meetings. And on the most perfect 75-degree spring days, Matt would sometimes wear a jacket over his scout shirt, lest he be embarrassed at being seen by the people in the one or two cars that might pass by.

When I would ask him about this, he'd tell me he wanted the jacket "in case it got chilly." This from the kid who still sleeps with his ceiling fan set to High in January. Few forces in nature are as powerful as the self-consciousness of the teenage boy.

Oh, well, can't win 'em all.

I intentionally left out a detail when I told the story of my becoming Scoutmaster: As I mentioned, Matt was then 12 years old and a relative newcomer to the troop (like most boys, he "bridged over" from Cub Scouts into Boy Scouts at age 11). I had always made an effort to be involved in the activities of both Matt and Megan, and had spent many years co-coaching their sports teams, so they were used to having me around.

But the Scoutmaster position was an entirely different level of involvement and authority, and it was important to me that my accepting the position wouldn't put Matt in an uncomfortable place with his fellow scouts. Sometime between the Monday night meeting, where I started to fully understand that I was going to be asked, and the Tuesday night meeting where the deal went down, I went to him and told him where I thought the situation was headed. I said I was willing to accept the Scoutmaster job if they asked, but only if it was okay with him. He thought it over for a moment and said it was fine.

Seeing those words on the page now, one could question the wisdom of giving veto authority over a very important and delicate situation to a 12-year-old. But we were involved in scouting for Matt's benefit, not mine, and if being the Scoutmaster's kid was going to negatively affect his enjoyment of the experience, I wanted no part of it.

With Matt's buy-in, it did indeed all turn out well. We shared bonding experiences that any father would envy, camping and hiking and traveling together on the Florida Sea Base and Yellowstone trips as well as many weekend outings. And best of all, five years later the buttons popped off my shirt one by one as we all celebrated Matt's achievement of the Eagle Scout rank. (For his Eagle Project, he solicited donations of used musical instruments for the Baltimore City Public Schools, accumulating more than 200 items.)

I can only imagine what it would have been like if I had forged ahead and Matt had resented being scouting's equivalent of the Preacher's Kid. I do know it wouldn't have been much fun for him or me.

Parenting and management are not the same thing, but this is one parallel that absolutely works: Whatever the initiative, you'll have a much easier go of it when the team buys into it first.

The other vital parenting/management lesson I learned from Matt's time in scouting: sometimes the very best thing you can say to someone... is nothing.

Case in point: As previously noted, Boy Scouts was not for me as a youth. In hindsight, this probably had more to do with the transition from my den of Cub Scouts to a troop of older, unfamiliar boys than it did with the scouting program itself. Whatever the reason, scouting and I didn't click, not even a little.

And so it was that when Matt's turn came I pretty much expected him to have the same reaction. While he loved Cub Scouts, he is, after all, very much like me in many ways, so my private prediction was that he would not stick with scouting for very long once he bridged over.

The key word there is "private." In one of my smartest moves as a parent, I was careful to keep that opinion to myself, and tried very hard not to let my own experience color Matt's feelings about scouting. In short, I stayed out of the way and let him make up his own mind.

You know the rest. Our son the Eagle Scout loved everything about Boy Scouts (except for wearing his uniform in public). And even better, I had a front-row seat for some of his most memorable experiences as a teen.

In fact, as a parent I can't think of any other activity that would have allowed us to spend that much time together. Think about it: By the time they're of high-school age, just about all our kids' activities revolve around school: sports, drama, band or chorus, clubs... they cease being ours for very large chunks of time. And Matt was involved in many of those things, but we also got to sit around a lot of campfires together. The world would be a better place if people spent more time sitting at a fire... There's something mesmerizing about staring into the ever-changing light show in the embers, especially after a long day of hiking.

In our case, the magical power of a campfire had an unintended side effect: After a while, Matt would sort of forget I was there and I could watch him with his hair down, so to speak, laughing and joking and bonding with his fellow scouts in a completely unguarded way. It was the teenage boy equivalent of watching animals in their natural habitat, and it's one of my warmest memories of that time (campfire pun intended).

What a joy for a dad that was, and all because I had the good sense to keep my mouth shut as Matt began his scouting career.

Lesson: Sometimes the very best thing you can do as a leader is be quiet and stay out of the way.

Scoutmaster Minute
LEADER OR FOLLOWER?

There were two speeches in the news today. The one you probably heard about was President Obama's address to the nation's students, and I thought that what he said was a good message for students—or Scouts—starting a new year: Set goals, and work hard to achieve them. This is a great time to set your goals for the Scouting year and figure out what you need to do for that next rank or what Merit Badges you want to earn.

The speech you probably didn't hear about was in Philadelphia, where Michael Vick spoke at a high school. You know the story: He was the highest-paid player in the NFL until he was arrested for organizing a dog-fighting ring. He spent about 18 months in federal prison, and now he's trying to make a comeback as a backup with the Eagles.

I thought that what he said today was noteworthy: For all of the money he was paid to be a leader on the field, he was too much of a follower off it. And obviously he was following the wrong people.[8]

So the question is: If a guy who's 10 or 12 years older than most of you—with enough money to do anything he wants—can't resist peer pressure, where does that leave you?

You're at an age where you're still figuring out who you're going to be, and you'll find yourself in situations where the people you're with want to do something you know is wrong. It's called peer pressure for a reason… it takes strength to resist and to say: "I don't care if my friends make fun of me or call me names, I'm not going to do that."

We talk a lot about leadership here at Scouts, and there's one pretty good definition: sometimes being a leader means knowing when not to be a follower.

THE AGE OF THE HOME RUN

I find myself watching baseball less and less as the years go by, and not just because my beloved Orioles have embarked on a multi-year rebuilding process after setting new standards for ineptitude over the past couple of seasons.

No, I seem to care less about the game because it's changed pretty dramatically over the years, away from the "small ball" components of the game like bunting, stealing bases, hit-and-run plays... the strategy that made it interesting. Instead, we get a bunch of guys with terrible-looking uppercut swings trying to jack the ball into the stands. Sometimes they do, with prodigious results, but it fails to hold my interest.

Baseball isn't alone, of course. The NFL has become pass-happy, NBA players rain down 3-pointers from different ZIP codes, and holes on PGA golf courses that used to demand a 5-iron for the second shot are now seeing guys like Dustin and Rory bomb their drives 380 yards and grab a pitching wedge. And as a guy who hits it about 180, and usually into the woods, this disturbs me to no end.

On TV, we're treated to "reality" shows (perhaps the most inappropriate term in the history of the English language) where homes are flipped and transformed into palaces, all in the span of 22 minutes plus commercials. Entrepreneurs pitch ideas to the sharks and walk away with millions in funding in mere moments, and 20-something couples with $900k budgets let us follow along on their search for just the right home. Watch enough sports coverage and you'll see a commentator say, with a straight face, that a certain NFL free agent is a bargain at *only* $12 million per year.

We live in the age of the home run.

I risk venturing into You-kids-get-off-my-lawn territory here ("When I was your age, baseball players wore high socks, ran out ground balls and made $350 a year!"), but here's the point: Add all this up, and throw in the highlight-reel social media environment we already covered, and we've arrived at a very distorted view of success. It's a right now, all-or-nothing proposition.

In the Internet Age everything is available instantly. We can read, watch or listen to virtually any book, movie or song right now. So why should we wait for… well, anything? We're not being conditioned to put in the work that leads to success in business or even in our personal relationships. No wonder we seem so collectively unhappy.

Everyone's out there trying to hit the home run, launch the startup that will attract the 7-figure investors, land the "whale" account that will dwarf all the others, or become the next Kardashians or Real Housewife of Wherever.

But you know what? There are plenty of other ways to measure success, and—this is something that comes up frequently in my business roundtable group—you can do really well as a consistent singles-hitter. Even singles-hitters occasionally put one in the seats, but if you consider anything less to be a failure you're setting yourself up for a lot of misery.

Of course, that approach requires the courage to not follow the crowd.

I recently had a protracted and unpleasant encounter (involving my daughter and a lease) with another set of parents who have achieved a level of wealth with which I will never be familiar, short of a winning Powerball ticket: a 30,000-square-foot house (with four, count 'em *four*, living rooms), membership at a country club that has hosted several U.S. Opens... you get the idea. And I can tell you that based on this experience at least, the rich are definitely *not* happier than the rest of us. Across a span of two months, we tussled over an amount that I'm certain was less than their monthly food-and-beverage minimum at The Club (but enough to keep me awake at night), and more dishonest, difficult and miserable folks you have never encountered. If you think massive wealth will make all your troubles go away, think again.

I think we collectively need to get over the idea that the only worthy outcome is the slam-dunk, home-run, overnight-success model. It's not a matter of settling for less; it's a matter of being true to ourselves and recognizing the gross distortion in the view of success we get from our electronic devices. In other words, to not follow the crowd.

There's no doubt that I could have been wealthier if I'd made some different career decisions along the way, but wealth does not equal success. When I look at the bigger picture I see modest financial success, work that I love with unmatched schedule flexibility and relatively low stress levels, generally good health, 30 years of happy marriage and two grown children who are becoming amazing adults. And that last bit may have something to do with those career choices that allowed my wife and me to be involved parents, volunteers, coaches and yes, a Scoutmaster. I wouldn't trade all that for *two* 30,000-square-foot houses.

What would you do with four living rooms anyway?

Scoutmaster Minute
INSPIRATION ON THE TRAIL

Sometimes life hands you a lesson in the strangest places…

There we were on Saturday *[on a hiking trip in an all-day downpour]* on the Appalachian Trail with the rain falling harder and harder, covered in ponchos and trash bags, the smaller guys having a hard time keeping up… The map showed a shelter ahead, and we decided to stop there, have lunch and plan our next move.

When we got to the shelter, a dog was barking at us. She and a few hikers were already occupying the shelter, but they made room for us to get out of the rain. Then one of the hikers struck up a conversation. He was from Georgia, and was hiking the trail from one end to the other. He had started in Maine, and his stories made us feel like sissies… he had climbed virtually straight uphill through gushing rainwater, had been literally blown over by the wind, had hiked through one of the rainiest seasons on record in New England.

On top of all that, he was a cancer survivor. He'd had Stage 4 cancer and had returned to health only a year and a half ago. I looked at his website he'd told us about, and it said that when he was too weak from chemotherapy to do anything else, he would surf the internet for photos of hikers on the Appalachian Trail. And that was his motivation to get well enough to finish his journey.

All that was inspirational enough, but before he told us any of that he had a message for us, and it was *how many good people there are in the world*. Before we heard about his struggles on the trail or his illness, he told us about all the people who had helped him along the way: fellow hikers, people bringing him groceries at trail crossings, and so on. And that was so refreshing to hear, because *good* doesn't make the news. Turn on the TV, pick up a newspaper, look at the internet and all you'll see are stories of people doing horrible things to each other, and it's easy to forget that there's still a lot of good being done.

As a Scout, you're part of that good: cheerful, courteous, kind, doing a good turn daily; and that's an uplifting thought to end our meeting.

A FEW WORDS

I wish I could say I had ever inspired anyone the way that hiker moved us on that rainy day. What a story to tell: cancer survivor, incredible physical struggles on the trail, and what did he lead with? People are good.

Just wow.

That Scoutmaster Minute doesn't fully describe the conditions that day. We started out in steady rain that gradually got heavier… and heavier… and just when you thought it couldn't rain any harder, it did. That section of the Appalachian Trail was literally a torrent of water when we stepped off to regroup. And somehow that made the encounter even more unexpected and moving. In mere moments, a few short words turned a bad morning around and made an impression that still lingers.

It wasn't the first or last time that a few short words would turn out to be pivotal.

In perhaps my second year as Scoutmaster, one of my older scouts, Leon, and I were chatting as we were setting up for a troop meeting. He was then beginning his junior year of high school, so I knew it was time to start thinking about colleges.

Leon was the son of divorced Chinese parents. His father had remained in China, where Leon would visit him for several weeks every summer, while his mother came stateside and married an American. Leon was bright, studious and polite, and the owner of a quirky sense of humor (on one winter camping trip he decided that a simple snowman wasn't worthy of his attention and instead built a snow llama, quite the engineering feat).

On this particular day, just for the sake of conversation, I asked Leon what he was thinking about his college choices, more in the sense of his interests in a major, not a particular school. He rattled off a couple of possibilities and then asked, "What do you think I should do, Mr. Rafferty?"

A little surprised that he would be interested in my advice, I responded just as you probably would have: "I don't know, Leon. What do you *like* to do? What interests you?" I'm a little embarrassed to admit that I don't remember the rest of the conversation; it was just a quick, off-the-cuff chat, and in fact I forgot that it had taken place.

I forgot, that is, until about a year and a half later. Upon reaching his Eagle Scout rank, Leon sent me a handwritten thank-you note (another thing to love about scouting; I have the nicest collection of actual ink-on-paper, personal notes). In the note he thanked me for my leadership and for my help in his getting to Eagle, and then he specifically recalled that conversation. Leon wrote that it was the first time ever that anyone had asked him what *he* wanted to do with his life.

As American parents of American kids in the 21st century, that's a little hard to wrap our minds around, isn't it? We let our little darlings steer the ship in many ways, sometimes to a fault. But there it was. An offhand question, all of six words ("What do you like to do?"), but it made a difference.

Flash back now to the summer before our troop tragedy and my sudden promotion to Scoutmaster: As previously noted, I was without a position in the troop, and hoped to keep it that way. I did make an effort, however, to get out and help on our camping trips when I could, just to be an extra set of hands, because we were always short of drivers and chaperones.

And so it was that I found myself at Camp Heritage, not far from Pittsburgh, helping to cover the second half of our troop's week away at summer camp. Every Boy Scout troop goes to summer camp for a full week each year, often at some distance from home. The program at summer camp allows each boy to pursue the merit badges he needs and/or wants, so the boys are all on their own schedules and come and go from the troop's campsite all day long. There needs to be an adult at the campsite at all times to supervise, and it was always difficult to find moms or dads who could help out during the week, so there I was, burning a few vacation days.

I arrived on Wednesday at around midday, and as luck would have it, Matt didn't have any classes right after lunch, so he agreed to take me on a walking tour of the camp and show me where all the important things were, like the mess hall, showers and trading post (usually a combination of gift shop and junk food emporium).

To fully appreciate this story, you need to understand two things: One, our son is a man of few words; and Two, if there were an Olympic gold medal for understatement, I would have just won it with statement One. Matt has always been a guy who never uses a whole word when a syllable will do, and has never been one to share his feelings or say much about what's going on inside (Says my wife: "I wonder where he gets *that*."). Which makes what happened next all the more remarkable.

As we headed back to the troop campsite, I said something to Matt right out of the Dad Playbook, like: "Well, I'm glad I could come up and spend some time with you, bud." He replied, "I'm glad, too." He could have stopped right there... my day was made, if not my week.

But we walked a few more strides and, referring to the other boys in the troop, he turned to me and said, "You're one of their favorite leaders."

This startled me, because I was *not* a leader, didn't want to *be* a leader and certainly would not use that term to connect myself in any way with Troop 328. I thought, and perhaps said, "Well, that's nice," and that was that.

Until the following February, when it became apparent that I was going to be asked to step up and lead those same boys through the aftermath of this unthinkable tragedy.

As I struggled with my decision, as I worried over my lack of relevant experience, and ultimately as I sat facing the 11 committee members in that room on a Tuesday night, I remember Matt's words coming back to me. And I remember thinking: "Maybe what these young men need right now is someone they *like*, someone they're comfortable with, someone they feel they can talk to, because we have a lot of healing to do. And maybe that's more important in this moment than having someone who knows three ways to start a fire without matches."

Again, six words: "You're one of their favorite leaders."

I don't want to take more credit than is due; Leon is extremely bright and capable, and he would have succeeded at whatever he chose to do, whether or not our conversation had ever taken place. But if those words didn't change a life, they at least changed a perspective. And Matt? His six words indisputably changed one life (mine) and arguably changed quite a few others.

Again, you might ask, "So what? What does any of this have to do with me, or with business?" And I would answer your question with another, rhetorical, question: How much time, effort and money do we spend chasing the elusive thing we call company culture, and its first cousin, employee engagement?

The things we say to those around us matter, and they especially matter when those hearing our words are the people we lead, in business or at home. What you may think is a throwaway comment or a joke can be taken to heart in ways you never expected. Sometimes that's a good thing, as in these examples. And sometimes it's not.

If there were a Mount Rushmore of business literature authors, Tom Peters would undoubtedly be carved into it. As you probably know, he's a keen student of corporate excellence and its elusive sibling, company culture.

In "The Excellence Dividend," Peters says:

Culture is shaped by the casual comment the boss makes to the receptionist as she walks through the door in the morning.

Culture is shaped by three casual comments—no more than thirty seconds each—that the boss makes as she walks the twenty-five yards from the receptionist's desk to her office.

Culture is shaped dramatically by the tone and quality and care put into the six emails the boss responds to in the fifteen minutes after she gets to her desk.

Culture is shaped by every twitch and blink and comment the boss makes at the morning meeting.[9]

If you are any kind of a leader in a business setting, I guarantee you've spent some time thinking about your company's culture. You might even have convened groups to address the culture or brought in

---

9   Tom Peters, The Excellence Dividend: Meeting the Tech Tide with Work that Wows and Jobs that Last (Vintage, 2018)

outside help. But I wonder whether you've considered the words that leave your own mouth as the seeds from which that culture will sprout.

One final note: In the examples here I've largely been concerned with the spoken word. But note what Peters says about the tone and quality of emails. It is extremely difficult to accurately convey tone in an email or instant message, and a note fired off in a hurry—hey, we're busy here—can easily be construed as brusque or even rude. Double-check what you've written, think twice before you hit Send, and follow up in person to make sure the message was not only received but interpreted as you intended. The last thing you want is a cheesed-off employee allowing resentment to fester over a misinterpreted comment. Worse, if you misstep here, chances are you'll be the last to know.

Scoutmaster Minute
AFTER YOU

What do all 12 points of the Scout Law have in common?

I think the common thread is that they're all about other people; a Scout is courteous, kind, etc.... to others. Even the points that don't seem that way: "A Scout is reverent" seems to be only about our own relationship with God, but part of reverence is respecting the religious beliefs of other people. And I guess if a Scout is clean, he's taking pity on those around him...

Scouting is one of the few places where you get reminded of this, and it's important because our culture has become very self-centered. If you turn on your TV, you get show after show of people with cameras pointed at them talking about me, me, me, me, me. If you go on Facebook no one asks, "How are you?" They say, "I'm doing my homework" or "look at my meal" (or like the commercial... "I'm... sitting... on... the... patio.").

And when you start to drive, you'll really appreciate how self-centered we all seem to be, because there are days when it seems like everybody on the road just wants you out of the way because their time is way more important than yours and they're going to get there first!

So, the Scout Law reminds us to put others first. It's really 12 different ways of looking at the Golden Rule. And we're reminded to Do a Good Turn Daily to help us make a habit of putting other people's needs ahead of our own. And that's a good thing, because someone putting aside their own needs to do something for others is really the only way our world ever gets better.

I'M SORRY THAT HAPPENED

O ne more story about the power in the words we use: This predates my scouting career by a few decades, but I'm including it here because the lesson I learned has stayed with me for all these years.

At the start of my sophomore year as a Radio-TV Communications major at Ithaca College in central New York state, I applied for a part-time announcer position at a commercial radio station in town… and got it. My radio career was officially launched at age 18, and I was feeling pretty good about myself.

WHCU-AM and FM occupied the second floor of a building on the Commons in downtown Ithaca, upstairs from a chain restaurant. Owned by Cornell University (the "CU" in the call letters), but operated as a commercial enterprise, the two stations were an amazing training ground for a newbie. In typical small-market radio fashion, the format depended somewhat on the time of day. The AM station was largely

128

an MOR (middle-of-the-road) music station, with hourly network news updates. The FM station was classical music by day and an urban-oriented music format called Nightsounds after dark. And between the two, they broadcast most of the major Cornell sporting events: football, basketball, lacrosse, hockey and so forth. It could not have been a more diverse or challenging learning environment.

The commercials were on tape cartridges ("carts" in radio parlance); most of the music was on actual vinyl records that had to be cued up on a turntable; and—wait for it—we announcers chose our own music. On the AM side, the format we had to follow was pretty complex: male vocal, female vocal, group vocal, instrumental, repeat. The telephone in the office reception area had about a 50-foot cord on it so it could be moved into the studios on weekends… during the week, announcers had no communication with the outside world (this turns out to be important foreshadowing for the story that follows).

Until just a couple of years ago, I was still a part-time announcer at a Baltimore radio station, where all the audio is digitized and gets on the air by being loaded in sequence on a computer. There was almost no wiggle room to depart from the scheduled songs except during an evening requests show. And there was not only a phone, but listeners could text the studio as well, to say nothing of the two-way interaction of social media. Telling stories about my start in Ithaca makes me feel like I should be in the Smithsonian… and don't even get me started on editing tape recordings with a grease pencil and a razor blade.

But one story needs to be told, and so it shall: My normal work at the Ithaca station happened on weekend mornings, when I would show up at 5 am or so to turn on the transmitters and be the DJ for the morning hours. But at the very end of my sophomore year, I was asked to fill in on the AM station on a Friday morning in May. This would be the final thing I did before launching myself on the 4½-hour drive home to the suburbs of Philadelphia for the summer... I was all done with exams, the car was packed and I was ready to go.

I was scheduled to work from 10 a.m. until noon, which actually meant starting at 10:06 a.m., because the station carried the CBS network news at the top of every hour. On this day, however, the news was preempted.

The week before, eight U.S. servicemen had been killed when their helicopter crashed in a failed attempt to rescue the American hostages held in Iran. It was a tragic exclamation point on a very dark time in our nation's history, and one that ultimately spelled the end of the Carter administration.

But at 18 years old, I wasn't paying much attention to all that. I had heard the headlines, of course, but the self-absorption of the young male easily won out over any concerns about the news.

In lieu of the news broadcast on this May Friday, CBS was providing live coverage of President Carter's eulogy for the servicemen. This coverage had started about 10 minutes earlier, and ended about 5 minutes later, than the usual top-of-the-hour news. The gentleman who did the morning show made way for me to get set up and I went into my regular routine of stacking all my commercial carts for the first hour, choosing the first couple of songs and cueing them up on the two turntables (not just dating myself now but carbon-dating myself).

President Carter finished his speech, CBS summarized it and wrapped up, I hit the station ID and my first song, and we were off and running.

Until about 20 minutes later.

At that point the receptionist came in to tell me that the phones had been ringing nonstop (remember, no phone in the studio on weekdays). Then and only then did I realize what I had done, and to this day I will stand on a stack of bibles, look you in the eye and swear that it was not intentional.

The song I had chosen to launch the proceedings after this tragic moment in American history? It was Frank Sinatra singing "That's Life." The lyrics, as you may recall, begin like this:

That's life… you know what all the people say
You're riding high in April, **shot down in May…**

True story.

I don't remember how I got through the remaining 90 minutes of that shift. I do remember spending a good bit of it with my head down on the console, secure in the knowledge that my radio career had just died a premature death at the age of eight months. I felt absolutely terrible about what I had done and was certain that it would result in my termination—deservedly so.

And then something remarkable happened.

Expecting to find my boss, the program director, waiting for me when I was done, I instead found *his* boss, the general manager (for those of a certain age: Arthur Carlson, not Andy Travis). The GM, whose name was actually Rudy, found me in the hallway, put his hand on my shoulder and said this: "I'm sorry that happened to you. I know you didn't do it on purpose. Have a good summer, don't worry about it, and we'll see you back here in the fall."

"I'm sorry that happened to you."

As though I'd been hit by a falling tree limb or something instead of making the most boneheaded move in the history of boneheaded moves. Forty years later, I can still hear him saying the words (six words again, if you're keeping score), and can still feel my astonishment at the reprieve I'd been given. Talk about just a few words having an impact.

The easy and sensible thing for Rudy to do at that point would have been to show me the door. There was no shortage of Communications majors looking for a radio gig in that town or anywhere else. But not only did he not do that, he *assumed* that it was an accident... he didn't grill me about what I was thinking (or not), didn't threaten me with future reprisals, didn't even leave me twisting in the wind all summer with a "*maybe we'll hire you back in the fall... I'll think about it.*" He went straight to forgiveness.

Now: Think about the last time a subordinate of yours screwed up. How did you react? How could you have reacted?

In a competitive hiring environment where companies struggle daily to find and retain good people, it's fair to ask this: If you were one of those good people, wouldn't you be more inclined to join or remain with a company where the culture was to go straight to forgiveness? Sure you would.

Employees who know they need not fear reprisal for every mistake are also more likely to do good things on their own. They're less afraid to do the outside-the-box things that make great companies great, and they're less likely to ask for help with every little task for fear of getting it wrong. When they do make mistakes—and we all do—they'll be more likely to own those mistakes and not try to hide them. In short, a culture of forgiveness equals a more empowered team, equals an improved company culture.

For our scouting adventure in the Florida Keys, we were divided into three crews of six people each: two adults and four scouts. Each crew had its own campsite (and its own schedule, more or less, though we did many activities together), and each crew prepared its own meals using ingredients supplied by the program.

After one long day of activities, our crew was starving. Blake had been appointed our crew leader, and it was his turn to work on dinner, which that night was a fairly simple pasta-and-sauce affair. We sat at our picnic table and chatted while Blake, with his back to us, hovered over the camp stove, a big pot of boiling water and noodles on one burner and a smaller one of spaghetti sauce on the other.

Out of the corner of my eye, I saw Blake pour the smaller pot of sauce into the larger pot of noodles, and although I hadn't been paying strict attention, something seemed a little off about it.

"Blake," I asked, "Did you drain the pasta first?"

He didn't reply, but the way his shoulders slumped gave me the answer. In his hunger and fatigue he had skipped a pretty critical step and poured the pasta sauce straight into the boiling water.

All of us being a little hangry from our day-long exertions by that point, it would have been easy for the other scouts—or even the adults—to go the "What on earth were you *thinking?*" route. But I was really proud that all of us were able to laugh it off. We had pink spaghetti that night… and of course, we never let Blake forget it.

There are some obvious lines of demarcation here: If an employee—or even a scout—has been asked to do, or not do, something nine times and the error is repeated a 10th, that's a very different conversation. But sometimes a mistake is just a mistake, no matter how bad it makes you or your company look in the short term (and I made that radio station look very bad on that day in May). Sometimes the very best thing you can do as a leader is to understand that the person who goofed might just feel worse about it than you do.

Try putting your hand on their shoulder and saying, "I'm sorry that happened to you." Odds are they'll never forget it.

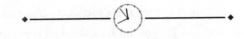

Scoutmaster Minute
NOT FOLLOWING THE CROWD

[Author's note: This references a somewhat-famous-in-scouting-circles letter written by "Dirty Jobs" star, Baltimore native and Eagle Scout Mike Rowe. A scout's father wrote to him asking if he could offer a little motivation to his son, who was close to reaching Eagle Scout rank but seemed to be losing interest. The non-sugar-coated reply is legendary.]

Last week I read you that letter from Mike Rowe, and it was pretty blunt, wasn't it? He says things like, "The Eagle Award isn't meant for those who have to be dragged across the finish line," and essentially tells the young man, "I have no idea whether you have what it takes to be an Eagle Scout."[10]

I asked you to think about that, and maybe your first thought was: "Well, Mr. Rafferty must be off his medication again, because Troop 328 does pretty well when it comes to our guys getting to Eagle rank." And

---

10   Mikerowe.com

you're right; we do. But there are just a few of you who perhaps could use a little verbal kick in the pants, and there it is.

The other thing that I think is so important in that letter doesn't necessarily have anything to do with being an Eagle Scout or even being a Scout. It's the part where he says: "The best decisions I've made in my own life are those decisions that put me on the outside of being cool."

I've spoken to you several times about peer pressure, because you're at the age where it really becomes a huge factor. And here is a very successful guy telling you that the best things in his life have happened when he went in a different direction from the crowd.

Now, sometimes going along with the crowd is fine; you should have friends, and you should do things together. But sometimes there's a better way, and you need to be able to recognize that and have the courage to go in a different direction. If you always follow the crowd, the only places you'll go are where everyone's already been.

THE PARADOX

I n Scouting as in business, a little tough love is called for from time
to time.

I've already described how that very difficult final year at the home
improvement company affected me individually, and it may have been
even more of a challenge as a manager. I was responsible for a residential
remodeling sales team of six, most of whom had more longevity at the
company than I did (and mind you, I was coming up on two decades
at that point).

Until then, the sales manager role had been more of a caretaker
position. Given the long track record of success most of the team had,
there was precious little I was going to teach them about selling. My
job was, as I liked to put it, to keep the trains running on time: tee up
their appointments, matching up customer with salesperson in the way
I felt would work best; check in with them on open opportunities to

make sure nothing was slipping through the cracks; that sort of general housekeeping.

But with new ownership came new ways of doing things, and for all my issues with the owner I would be lying if I said change wasn't needed at that point. The old ways had served us well when the economy was booming, but in the Great Recession, not so much. Leads were harder to come by and more precious than ever, and we could no longer afford to give any of them a halfhearted effort, knowing there'd be another one right behind it… because now, there wasn't.

To offer one example, our salespeople generally didn't work on Saturdays. If that was the only time someone could see us, we would find a way to make it work, but while just about every other company did Saturday appointments routinely, it was voluntary for our guys.

And so just as my role changed dramatically, so did nearly every procedure in the sales process, and needless to say, this did not always sit well with guys who'd been doing things more or less as they wished for a long, long time. I quickly assumed the role of the rope in a year-long tug-of-war between ownership and front-line sales. There was some stress and fraying, for sure.

Finally, I decided that what the team needed was a change of perspective, and that I would be the one to deliver it.

I had been reading "Good to Great" by Jim Collins, a staple of anyone's must-read list of business books, and I was fascinated by the chapter on the Stockdale Paradox. If you haven't read it, you should, but here's the condensed version:

Admiral James Stockdale (later to be Ross Perot's running mate in the 1992 presidential election) was the highest ranking officer at the "Hanoi Hilton," the infamous POW camp at the height of the Vietnam War. His exploits and leadership in the name of survival through his eight years in captivity were of staggering proportion, and again worthy of your time. But for our purposes, the Paradox:

Interviewed by Collins many years later, the admiral was asked how he kept hope for all those years, not knowing what the ending would be. He said that he never lost faith that some way, somehow, he would not only get out but would use the experience as the defining moment of his life.

So who didn't make it out? asked Collins next. "The optimists," said Stockdale. These were the ones who repeatedly said, "We'll be out by Christmas," or some other date, and as enough of those milestones came and went, "they died of a broken heart."

Well, wait, didn't they have faith also? Yes, but it was a faith that *ignored the reality of their situation.*

Stockdale concluded:

"This is a very important lesson. You must never confuse faith that you will prevail in the end—which you can never afford to lose—with the discipline to confront the most brutal facts of your current reality, whatever they might be."[11]

What a wonderful, subtle distinction. And how absolutely perfect it was at that moment. This was the message I would share with the sales team. And so I got to work.

I read and reread that section of the book, and I practiced the presentation I would give at our Friday sales meeting for more than a week, delivering it out loud at every opportune private moment and polishing, polishing, polishing.

The day of the meeting came, and once our usual housekeeping was complete, I launched into the presentation for the sales staff (and the owner), painting with words the ordeal of Admiral Stockdale, the paradox of keeping faith but not ignoring reality, and concluding:

"This company has new ownership. That is a reality that's not going away. The economy isn't doing well, and for the time being at least,

---

11 Jim Collins, Good to Great: Why Some Companies Make the Leap and Others Don't (HarperBusiness, 2001)

that's another reality for us. And the things that are expected of you have changed as well, and that is yet another cold, hard fact. I have faith that we are all capable of making great things happen here, and I hope you do too, but don't for one second think that's going to happen by doing things the old way. Those days are gone."

It was really the first time the whole situation has been crystallized for them in that way, and I felt I had finally made an impression. In my mind at least, I had struck just the right tone between optimism for the future and the come-to-Jesus talking-to that the circumstances demanded. My plan had been to dismiss the meeting immediately thereafter and send the team out the door with that as a final thought (like a Scoutmaster minute for grownups), hoping they would then reflect upon it and begin to change some old behaviors.

That was the plan.

What actually happened, however, was quite different. The owner clapped his hands together and said, "That was great. Really well done. And by the way, we're all going to start working on Saturdays."

The room erupted. Another 20 minutes of general discord, punctuated by threats of quitting, followed before we could settle things back down, and even then, the salespeople were seething as they left. And all the good I thought I might have accomplished was undone—and worse—that quickly.

Within the hour, I was in the owner's office laying into him in a way I had never done before (true to form, he had not shared with me, the manager of the affected salespeople, his plan to make this change). I didn't scream or yell, but I was visibly upset as I recounted how hard I had worked to prepare that presentation, what I was trying to accomplish, and the good it might have done had he not chosen that moment to lob his ill-considered hand grenade into the middle of the room. I got a half-hearted apology that I'm pretty sure did not contain the word "sorry," followed by some snide remark about my "needing a hug." He truly was one of a kind… fortunately.

Consider the distinction of the Stockdale Paradox for a moment in your own life. You may have absolute faith that, for example, your financial situation will improve. But if that faith is based on the expectation of a winning Powerball ticket and not the work that goes into a concrete plan to achieve financial independence, you're very likely to be disappointed.

The irony in my story, of course, was this: I was so concerned about bringing the sales team around that I never considered the Stockdale Paradox as it applied to me. Clearly, I was still in full denial of my own situation, still believing everything would work out if I just kept grinding. I had *faith*, but not the *discipline* to accept the reality that I was no longer wanted there. Two months later I was gone.

Scoutmaster Minute
INTEGRITY

A Scout is trustworthy... you hear the word "integrity" a lot, and I suppose there are a lot of ways to define it. Here's one:

Back in November, a golfer named J.P. Hayes was playing in a tournament, attempting to qualify for the PGA Tour this year. For those of you who don't follow golf, let me explain: The PGA Tour is like the major leagues of golf; there are several other tours that are more like the minor leagues. If you get on the PGA Tour you can finish 30th all year long and make a few million dollars... on the other tours, you sleep in your car a lot. So, needless to say, it's extremely competitive, with a lot of golfers trying to qualify for just a few slots each year.

So J.P. Hayes was playing in this qualifying tournament when he got to the 3rd hole... and when he went to mark his ball on the green he realized that it was not the ball he had started his round with. That's a violation of the rules... but nobody knew except him.

So what did he do? He called a Rules official over and said, "This is not same model of ball I started the round with. I'm assessing a two-stroke penalty on myself." Now, two strokes could easily make the difference between success and failure, so that was a big deal. But the story doesn't end there...

When he returned to his hotel that evening, he thought about it a bit more and realized that the second ball was a prototype... it had not yet been put on the market or officially approved for play. Once again, a violation of the rules; and once again, nobody knew but him. So what did he do? He went back the next morning and disqualified himself from the tournament, virtually ending any chance he might have had of being on the tour this year.

There are a lot of ways to define integrity, and I think J.P. Hayes gives us a great example of one of them: doing the right thing *even when no one else is watching.*[12]

Scoutmaster Minute
INTEGRITY, PART II

I was in a store up in Pennsylvania the other day, sort of a general purpose variety store. There were a few checkout counters, and they were fairly busy, with maybe two or three people in each line.

The woman in front of me had a single item (an outdoor thermometer), and she waited for one person ahead of her with a fairly big order to check out. When her turn came, she put the thermometer on the counter and said to the cashier, "I just checked out a few minutes ago, but this wasn't on my receipt. I think you forgot to ring it up."

Now, a Scout is trustworthy, but there's trustworthy and then there's *trustworthy*. I found myself wondering whether I would have taken the trouble to come back into the store and wait in line again to pay for a $4 item if that had been me.

What would you have done?

INTEGRITY

W hy do we have to teach integrity? Are we really wired to do the wrong thing and destined to spend our lives fighting those natural, dishonest impulses?

It sure seems that way if you watch the news, doesn't it? Locally, Baltimore seems to be a breeding ground for corrupt politicians, and we're mere miles north of Ground Zero for the truth-challenged, our nation's capital. Of course, dishonesty isn't limited to politics, as evidenced by the revelation that the Houston Astros were aided in their run to the World Series in 2017 by a coordinated effort to steal the other teams' signs. And there's always plenty of shame to spread around in the corporate world.

Honesty doesn't make headlines, of course. Plenty of people spend their days doing the right things, but you won't see it on TV. Just as social media can distort our view of success, watching the news would lead us to believe that just about everyone is crooked.

Integrity was a regular topic in our Scoutmaster Minutes because it's an obvious pillar of the scouting program, and because I felt it was something our young men needed to hear about regularly as they passed through their teenage years and ran the gauntlet of peer pressure that comes with the territory. Those are indeed the years when many of our habits are formed, for better or worse.

We were blessed with a great group of young men who had been taught the difference between right and wrong long before they became Boy Scouts. But teenagers are teenagers, and we still had our moments here and there when temptation was stronger than willpower.

While we were away for summer camp one year, one of the boys reported his new pocketknife missing from his tent. There had been some minor bad blood between him and one of the other scouts, and everyone—including the adult leaders—was pretty sure who was responsible. It presented an interesting leadership decision: quietly confront the presumed culprit or sit back and see how it played out? Confident that we had enough adult eyes on the situation that it wouldn't devolve into a "Lord of the Flies" reboot, I elected to wait and watch.

Lo and behold, a day later the prime suspect "found" the missing knife in the woods not far away. He saved face, sort of, and by not calling him out we kept a bad situation from getting uglier.

Of course, there's much more to integrity that the absence of lying or stealing, and doing the right thing is not always a binary yes-or-no choice. The stakes also get much higher when we move the conversation toward the world of business. Now we have our careers, and by extension our families, on the line, and the temptations to bend the rules are far greater than a shiny new pocketknife. We have dozens of moments in any given day where we choose exactly how honest to be, or how much to shade the truth (and hide the flaws) in a sales presentation or a job interview… and few of us get them all right.

Just a few months into my consulting career, I was thrilled to land a very large engagement with a local company. It was a ton of work with a wide-ranging scope and a monthly number to match... and it came to an end after less than six months. Looking back on it, the client was less reasonable and more demanding than most, so the fault was not all mine. But I had to admit to myself that in my eagerness to bring the deal home I had agreed to some deliverables that really were not in my wheelhouse. Unsurprisingly, those parts of the arrangement did not go very well, and the client had legitimate reasons to be unhappy. Had I been honest with myself and them about what I was really capable of at the time of the proposal, I would have handled things differently to take on less work for a lower figure. That misstep still bothers me.

Integrity is not a thing that we have or don't have, it's a habit and a process that we revisit every single day, trying to do better than yesterday and still better tomorrow. And we can't be honest with others until we're honest with ourselves.

Scoutmaster Minute
THREE GUIDELINES

I had a conversation a few weeks ago with the father of a young man from another high school in the area. In the course of our chat he told me that he has three things he asks his children to do: 1) raise your hand once a day in each of your classes; 2) do something nice for someone else every day; 3) meet someone new each week.

I like these guidelines because they're all about developing habits, and by now you know that's one of my favorite topics.

If you're not already raising your hand once a day in each class, think about it, because doing so turns you from a spectator to a participant in your own education, and I think you can guess which one of those choices will have a better result.

"Do something nice for someone else every day..." Well, we're Scouts, and we call that "doing a good turn daily." I'm sure you guys already do this, and probably don't even think about the fact that you're doing it, but it never hurts to be reminded: We should all be finding a way to make someone else's day a little better every day.

The third one, "meet someone new once a week," is probably the trickiest one for guys your age. Note that it doesn't say, "make a new best friend each week," just "meet someone." If you can manage to do that, what happens is that the person you meet will introduce you to other people, who will introduce you to other people, and so on, and pretty soon you'll have a very large circle of friends and acquaintances.

HEADS UP

As you've already read, I was fortunate enough to visit some amazing places over those scouting years, from Yellowstone National Park to the Grand Canyon to chunks of the Appalachian Trail in several states. Monica and I still regularly hike a beautiful wooded trail that's no more than five minutes from our home, taking on a reasonably challenging three-mile loop.

Needless to say, when you hike in places like those, the trails aren't paved. The surfaces range from smooth, hard-packed dirt to ankle-breaking rocks… to underwater, as in our Yellowstone adventure. There's always a root or a rock waiting to send you pitching face-first into the ground, so you need to keep an eye on your next steps at all times.

And therein lies the problem: It's very easy to be so concerned about your footing that you never lift your head up and appreciate the scenery all around you. It takes a little discipline to remember to soak in your surroundings once in a while, so your only memories of the outing aren't of the dirt beneath your feet. Not only that, but if your eyes are always focused three feet in front of you, it's very easy to miss the trail markers and wind up somewhere you did not intend to be.

Those markers can range from obvious to almost nonexistent. Some trails are marked with professionally lettered signs (not that it always helps... read on), some with blazes of colored paint on a tree every so often, and where there are no trees, as in the Grand Canyon, we learned to look for cairns, small piles of rocks left by other hikers to show the way.

About those signs: Monica and I hiked a portion of the Appalachian Trail in Maryland one weekend. (Do we know how to celebrate an anniversary or what?) On the Sunday morning portion of the trip, perhaps 45 minutes after setting out, we realized we were headed into someone's backyard, a pretty good indicator that we were no longer on the trail. Fortunately, the homeowner was outside with his dog, and we were apparently not the first ones to have made that mistake. He gave us directions to bushwhack through his property and back to the trail, and we were soon back in the right place.

When we returned to where we had started, we spent a moment trying to figure out where we had gone wrong. And guess what? No more than 300 yards from where we had begun there was a large wooden sign overhead that said:

APPALACHIAN TRAIL

⬅

... and we had both missed it completely because our heads were down. Thank goodness I wasn't leading a scout troop that day... talk about embarrassing.

Now think about your daily work routine. Chances are that it's an endless succession of emails to be answered, maybe even actual phone calls... and your Hydra of a to-do list, with every completed task being replaced by two new ones.

Those are the roots and rocks of our workdays, aren't they? We have to keep our head down and get them done, because we surely will be tripped up if we don't. But if we're always focused on the next step, we miss the bigger picture... and it's very easy to take a wrong turn.

I'm a little biased, but I think this especially is a pitfall for the solo entrepreneur... we don't have a team around us to do the grunt work so we can keep an eye on our surroundings and correct our overall direction. If we don't see it ourselves, it doesn't get seen, and we have only our own judgement to tell us if we're headed the right way.

But even if you lead a large team, the trap of being caught up in the to-do's and the details of the workday is always waiting. As a leader, *you* need to be the one with your eye on the horizon to make sure you collectively don't miss the next signpost. That means forcing yourself to get out of the weeds, stop putting out the brush fires that pop up every day and make time for reflection and planning.

There's more than one way to do this, of course: I have a client who takes a nice trip to a tropical destination annually. Notice that I didn't say "vacation." No, he uses the time to sit on the beach or by the pool with his laptop, churning through a bunch of spreadsheets. And he gets some strange looks from other visitors, for sure. But he's reviewing his bigger picture: looking at where he's been, strategizing and setting goals for the year to come. And it bothers him not one bit that he's not vacationing in the traditional sense, because he knows it's time well spent.

When I found myself out of work and contemplating the entrepreneurial path for the first time, I reached out to just about every business contact I had ever known to see if they'd be willing to sit down over a coffee. This was not a huge list... if I had it to do over again, I would have invested much more time in networking when I still had a "real job." It turns out that "meet someone new once a week" is great advice in the business world also.

Not only were the vast majority willing to take time to sit down and talk, they were incredibly helpful and supportive of my business plan, which was a pretty vague thing at that point. One acquaintance who owned a small ad agency went so far as to share his legal agreements and other documents with me to give me a head start there, an incredibly generous gesture.

So Lesson One as an entrepreneur was this: People are ready and willing to help you on your journey, and to a degree that will likely surprise you.

Lesson Two: I needed to meet Mike.

I had heard Mike's name a few times over the years and knew that he was my opposite number at a competitor, managing the sales team for a roofing and remodeling company. I wasn't sure how meeting him would actually be productive, but when for the fourth time someone across the table from me at all those coffees said, "You need to talk to Mike," I decided I really should reach out. I sent an email introducing myself and we agreed to meet for breakfast.

Timing is everything in life, they say, and so it was. It turned out that Mike was at that moment leaving his position and purchasing a business built around peer group meetings, rebranding it as INSIGHT. We spoke about my plans, we spoke about his plans, and the result was that one of my first actions as a new business owner was to join an INSIGHT group.

That remains probably the best single action I've taken as an entrepreneur. More than eight years later I'm still a member, and it has paid off on so many levels. I mentioned earlier how it works, but here's a little more detail:

One morning each month, 8 to 12 business leaders sit around a conference table and help address each other's challenges. Mike not only runs the business but facilitates the meeting for my group (a handful of other facilitators run groups as well). It is both very simple and very profound, as we develop relationships far, far deeper than those that grow out of typical networking activities. We know each other's work and each other's families, and we challenge each other to do better professionally and personally.

My participation has led directly to a great deal of business, and I'm not kidding when I say that that might be the least of the benefits. I get great advice from people who know and care about what I do, and especially in the early days of my journey, realizing that I was able to *offer* good advice to others was a huge confidence booster. In my first year and beyond, those meetings were fuel for the voice in my head that said, "You can do this."

And guess what? Now I devote *two* mornings a month to INSIGHT, because I've recently started facilitating my own group (another step out of my comfort zone if you're keeping track).

If you're going it solo, a peer group can not only offer the guidance you need, but also replace the personal interactions you'll miss by no longer being in an office with co-workers. And if you lead a larger team, the group is your way to get invaluable and unvarnished feedback outside the echo chamber of your own company environment.

In either case, or anywhere in between, that monthly meeting forces you to stop stamping out the daily brush fires and look at the horizon on a regular basis. It's the best way I know to make sure you don't miss the markers that will keep you on the right trail.

Whether you're a solo entrepreneur, leading a team of hundreds or anywhere in between, I firmly believe you will reap huge benefits when you seek out the power of the group.

Scoutmaster Minute
PERSONAL FINANCE

I got one of our credit card bills in the mail last week. It was a big one: we had been on vacation, so we charged a lot of stuff and the balance due was almost $1,100.

I noticed on that same bill that the bank that issues the credit card had very helpfully noted that I only had to make a minimum payment of about $10. What do you think would happen if I did that?

I found a calculator on the internet and checked: If I never used that card again so there were no additional charges and I paid only the minimum every month, it would take 146 months to pay it all off. That's a little over 12 years. Oh, and over that time it would cost me $1,245 in interest. So that original $1,100 would wind up costing almost $2,350.

A Scout is thrifty, and part of being thrifty is not buying things you can't afford. A credit card is a great convenience—especially in the age of online shopping—but you need to have the discipline to spend only what you can pay for. When you get to about college age, you'll start getting credit card offers in the mail, and you must understand that just because your bank says you can have a credit card with a limit of $10,000 doesn't mean you should. It's very easy to get into debt over your head... and very hard to get out.

Scoutmaster Minute
THE TEENAGE BRAIN

I've been reading a really interesting book about the teenage brain (adults, insert your own punch line here).

You see, guys, your behavior sometimes confuses the adults in your life because we've noticed that teenagers often get angry very quickly, have sudden mood swings, and sometimes don't stop to think things through before they do something (have you ever had a parent say to you: "What were you thinking?").

Well, this book attempts to explain your behavior by taking a look at what's going on in your head, literally. In fact, it's called, "Why Do They Act That Way?"[13] And without turning this into medical school let me see if I can explain one bit that I found very enlightening:

Your brain has different regions, and they mature at very different rates. So the part that says, "This will be great! Let's do it! Go, go, go!"

---

13   Dr. David Walsh, Why Do They Act That Way? (Atria Books, revised 2014)

and releases a bunch of hormones to get you all fired up, well, that part matures very quickly. Meanwhile, the part that says, "You know, this might not be the best idea... let's stop and think about it," develops much more slowly. So the result, as the book puts it, is that the typical teenage brain has the engine of a NASCAR vehicle... and the brakes of a bicycle.

If you need proof, you fellows who drive or who are about to drive, take a look at your car insurance. On paper you should be a much better driver than me. For example, you have better eyesight, better reflexes and so on. But you're going to pay two or three times as much as I do for your insurance. Why? Because teenagers have a history of not always stopping to think things through and make good decisions, and when you're behind the wheel that can have disastrous results.

I tell you all this for two reasons: First, believe it or not, I do remember a little bit about being a teenager, and I remember what it feels like when you're ping-ponging back and forth from happy to sad to angry and wondering, "What is going on with me?" Maybe it's reassuring for you to know that something *is* going on, and to some degree it's out of your control.

Secondly, you probably feel like you hear the word "no" a lot at home, right? Mom & Dad tell you your work needs to be done before you go out, or ask you to stop and think about something before you do it, or they want to know, "Where will you be? Who will you be with? When will we hear from you?" and that's no fun for you. Trust me... it's no fun for your parents, either.

Even if they've never thought about it in exactly that way, your parents understand on some level that you have this combination of NASCAR engine and bicycle brakes going on, and they understand that a big part of their job is to be those brakes until you learn to grow and use your own. They're modeling good decision-making for you so that you can learn how it's done, because that's how you'll grow up to be the person we all want you to be.

THE WHOLE PERSON

O f all the Scoutmaster minutes I delivered over five years, that one about the teenage brain was the only one that I shared with the parents via email the following day. The content obviously involved family relationships, and I wanted them to be aware of what had been said, thinking it might make for meaningful dinner-table conversation. I remember one response from a mom who thanked me for caring about "the whole person, not just the scout."

As I started my journey as Scoutmaster, I was painfully aware of two things: One, the boys weren't going to learn a lot of scout skills from me in the early going. And Two, if the troop was going to survive this tragedy, we were going to have to keep a very close handle on how things were going for each of them as individuals.

So, very early on, I resolved that I would do my best to know what was going on in their lives outside of scouting. This was not as calculated as it might sound here on the page; all of the adult leaders truly cared about these guys. It was more a matter of knowing that in order to heal, we had to keep talking, and that those conversations would be more meaningful if we all knew and trusted each other.

I therefore made it my mission to know every boy's interests outside of scouting: I knew what instrument they played in the band or what sports they were involved in or what colleges they were applying to, or all of the above. And when someone made the lacrosse team or successfully auditioned for All-County band or chorus or the Baltimore Ravens Marching Band (for real!), I made it a point to share the news with the group when we circled up at the end of our meetings.

Once a year I would take our updated troop roster and put every boy's birthday on my Google calendar, and at that same end-of-meeting time I would give a little shout out to those with birthdays in the coming week.

How long did all that take? Maybe 15 minutes to log the birthdays, and no extra time at all to engage the boys and talk about their lives: before or after meetings, during down time on a camping trip… there were ample opportunities for conversation.

And the compliment I received most often from parents over the years? You probably guessed. They intuited that the leadership team really cared about their sons not just as Boy Scouts, but as people.

While many of the Scoutmaster Minutes directly addressed the pillars of the scouting program (bravery, honesty and so forth), others were a bit outside the scouting box, ranging from the ones you just read about the emotions of the teenager and how not to handle having a credit card, to our elections and "recalculating" when life doesn't go as planned.

Can you see where this is going as it relates to our topic of your company culture? Do your employees have the same trust in you? If you're not the boss, do your co-workers?

With the caveat that I didn't have to worry about running afoul of HR by prying too deeply and you do, the surest way to get your team all rowing in the same direction is to make it clear that you care about them as people, not just for what they can for you during business hours. And you can't fake this… they'll sniff it out in a second (as the old joke goes, sincerity is the key… once you can fake that, you've got it made).

In "The Infinite Game," Simon Sinek says, "It's not the people doing the job, it's the people who lead the people doing the job who can make the greater difference… There is absolutely zero cost for a manager to take time to walk the halls and ask their people how they are doing… and actually care about the answers."[14]

A 2017 Gallup poll titled "State of the American Workplace" reached the same unsurprising conclusion: "Employees need to know that someone is concerned about them as people first and as employees second."[15]

In other breaking news, the sun rises in the east.

Now, if you run a company with 500 employees, you can't be expected to know all their kids' names and their hobbies. But you can know those things about the people who report to you directly, and you can make it exceedingly clear that you expect them to take the same approach with *their* direct reports, and so on down the line. For my money there is no truer maxim in business than the one that says, "People join companies. They quit bosses." And you know what? People quit bosses a lot less often if they know the bosses really care about them as human beings.

---

14 Simon Sinek, The Infinite Game (Portfolio/Penguin, 2019), 93
15 Gallup, "State of the American Workplace," 2017

Not a Scoutmaster Minute
BEST DAMN DAY OF MY LIFE

I was on the 14th green at Pine Ridge when the news came. Of *course* I was on the 14th green at Pine Ridge, the most beautiful spot on the course where we spent so many hours together. And not only was I there, I was hearing his voice telling me, "Read the break and double it," because the green on 14 will fool you.

The trees reflected off the glassy reservoir, the birds swooped, the sun set, my phone chimed… and he was gone. And I missed the putt to boot.

The first time you met Dick, you thought, "Wow. There goes the World's Greatest Salesperson." Probably you said something like, "Hey, how are you?" and he responded with a hearty, "Best Damn Day of My Life! Thank you for asking!"

It was always good for a laugh, but there were just a few times when I heard that exchange play out a little differently, and it was much more enlightening:

Dick: "Best damn day of my life!"

Other person: "Wow! Why is that?"

Dick: "Because *you* cared enough to ask."

And that's it in a nutshell, because when Dick was around it was never about him. He lit up a room, but he made sure you knew that *you* were the most important person in it.

Eventually you realized that unlike all the other extroverted salespeople you've crossed paths with, this wasn't just a face he put on at work. It was in Dick's DNA. He wasn't the World's Greatest Salesperson… he was a *great person*, which is both much simpler and a lot harder to pull off.

When I visited the hospice the other day, Dick's wife, Debe, told me how grateful they all were that their nephew had been there with them through the whole ordeal. As a medical professional, he was able to interface with the doctors and nurses in a way that they could not, but more than that… he brought pizza. He brought biscuits from Chik-Fil-A. Without being asked he stopped at Walmart and got a change of clothes for all the ladies, who had not planned on being at the hospital and hospice for days on end. To all that I responded, "He has the family gift."

That's what it was with Dick as well: the gift of knowing what you needed before you did and then making it happen. Your drink was never empty (and he remembered what it was without asking), your birthday never forgotten, and your kids always laughed or saw a magic trick or both. When we talk about someone "having a gift," we usually mean that they're good with numbers or can play an instrument well or have a great eye for decorating. But Dick's gift was a gift *to us*, the gift of a better day because he always knew the right thing to do or say, whatever the situation.

His sole mission in life was to make your day a little bit better, whether you were a stranger on the street, a friend, neighbor, or his wife, daughter, son-in-law or grandchild. Exhibit A here is the online memory book that's overflowing with stories of the lives he touched. If you were a client, he knew your dog's name and your wife's birthday, and probably vice-versa.

And if you were blessed as we were to live next door to Debe and Dick for two decades, you experienced the gift as a regular occurrence: the bottle of champagne on the counter the day we moved in; the sudden realization that he was out front cutting our grass or edging our yard or shoveling our snow… *again*; coming out at 5 in the morning to leave on vacation and finding a note on the windshield wishing us a great trip; the countless bags of Oreos dropped off for Megan for no other reason than that he knew they were her favorite. (The time he put Matt into a trash can headfirst was really just icing on the cake, and well deserved, I might add.)

I can't think of higher praise to offer than this, and it is the truth: All four of the Raffertys are better people because of that incredibly fortunate circumstance of living in the immediate orbit of Dick, Debe and their family.

So today kind of feels like the Worst Damn Day of My Life, thank you for asking. We are crushed by his loss, crushed for Debe and the girls and sons-in-law and grandkids, crushed as we stood by helplessly watching the dream of a beach retirement turn into a prognosis that shrank from years to days to hours before we could form the words to protest. It's really hard not to be more than a little angry at the universe right now, because surely the wrong number has been called this time.

And our collective days will be just a little less bright.

What we should be doing, of course, is thanking God or our lucky stars or whatever we believe in that we were fortunate enough to have him in our lives, but that's easier said than done right now, and... dammit, Sirius/XM, will you stop playing "Wish You Were Here?"

So we look for hope, and we find it in odd places: on the long, somber ride home from my final visit with him, I paused at a rest stop on I-95. In the time it took to walk from my car to the men's room, not one but two complete strangers struck up conversations, which has happened to me—let me count the times—*never*. And a total of 30 seconds of small talk brightened a really awful day just a little bit... and I knew right away that it wasn't an accident.

To the best of my knowledge, Dick went to church only for weddings and funerals, but I'm not sure I've ever known anyone, religious or not, who did a better job of living his life in a way that any faith would be proud of. What Would Jesus Do? What Would Dick Do? Probably the best way to tell the difference is that the latter would involve Rum Babas and a Jimmy Buffett song.

When it became apparent that all this was not going to end well, Dick's grandson, Jack, asked his mother, "Momma, what are we going to do without Jiba?[16] He makes everything *fun*."

Jack, believe me, we're all asking that same question. And here's what we're going to do:

First of all, we—the Rafferty family and everyone else who knew your grandfather—are going to be there for you, your sister, your cousins, your parents and aunt and uncle, and for Grammee. We're going to be there with hugs and love and laughs and tears and—most of all—the memories of how he *made everything fun*. Not just today, not just this week, but to keep his memory alive in you and in all of us for as long as we're all around.

And the second thing we can do—and the very best way to remember our Dick and your grandfather—is to live as he did: Let's try every day

---

16   As just a small window into the man's sense of humor, his grandchildren called
      him "Jiba," which is the Peruvian Spanish word for "speed bump."

to make everyone else's day a little better, whether they're a stranger at a rest stop or someone we share our house with. Let's connect with people and try to figure out what they need before they realize it themselves.

Maybe, once in a while, we can even make it the Best Damn Day of Their Life.

CONNECTING

As you have no doubt gathered by now, that was not a Scoutmaster Minute. It was a visceral reaction to the passing of my dear friend and former next-door neighbor.

For all our efforts toward positive thinking, sometimes the universe just doesn't want to cooperate. Dick and Debe retired to the beach in North Carolina over the winter, fulfilling a longtime dream, and cancer took him with shocking suddenness only a few months later.

When you write a book like this, you try hard to be a comforting voice and to have the answers a reader is looking for, but I'm still at a loss on this one, sorry.

And maybe that's the whole point: Bad things happen far too often, and for reasons that are well beyond our powers to comprehend. In an upside-down sort of way, that's even more of a reason to look for the positive and to celebrate the good things in our lives.

My father passed away suddenly on a Sunday afternoon when our son Matt was 8. When the news came, I had to pack up quickly and drive to the family homestead in the Philadelphia suburbs, and I vividly remember getting ready to leave and standing outside our front door, torn between the need to get to my mother and the need to console my son, who was understandably heartbroken (at 5 years old, Megan was still a bit too young to fully understand).

"I know how you're feeling," I said to Matt, "and it's okay to be sad. We've lost someone we love very much. But we're sad because your Pop-Pop was such an important part of our lives, and we have to try to be grateful for all the good times we had together. That's easy to say and hard to do, but that's our job right now." (That sounds like a lot to lay on an 8-year-old, I know. Matt was, and is, wise beyond his years.)

That line of reasoning, of course, is a pillar of many religions. We're to set our grief aside and celebrate our loved one going to a better place. We don't even have funerals anymore; we have "celebrations of life." And that's all great, but sometimes we don't feel much like celebrating. The loss, especially if it's sudden, leaves a hole in us that refuses to be filled.

Of course, there is no more striking example of that combination of shock and loss than the Browning family tragedy, which was the catalyst for nearly everything you've just read. That anyone should ever have to experience something like that, let alone the young people who comprised our troop, is incomprehensible. And the scout troop was but one of the many moons in the orbit of the Browning family; we had no monopoly on the stunned grief that rippled throughout the greater community.

Such tragedies drive us to ponder the bigger picture and to contemplate how we live our own lives, but it seems the effect is usually temporary. Life and all its nagging details continue to come at us every day, and while "live each day as though it were your last" has a great ring to it, the reality is that it's probably *not* our last. Tomorrow we'll have to deal with the consequences of what we did or didn't do today. Taking off for the islands or not paying your mortgage really works only if it *is* your last day.

So let's look for the incremental ways to be a little better every day: engaging with other people and seeing if we can make *their* day a little better, showing real gratitude for the good things in our lives, making sure we're the person our family needs us to be. Time heals all wounds, but so does living a better life.

The more I reflect on having known both John Browning and my neighbor, Dick, the more I think that the reason we miss certain people so much is because of their ability to connect with those around them, including ourselves. To those of us who aren't as polished at making those connections, it seems a rare gift indeed, and we dearly miss it when it's gone.

Why do the rest of us struggle with this? To some degree we can decide where we go in life and what we do, but there's a randomness to our encounters with other people, no matter how much we want there not to be. We can choose to attend a networking event or a church function, for example, but we can't control who else will show up.

Most of us love to be in control, or to think we are, and all that randomness can make us ill at ease. Discomfort with networking events is a perennial topic in my business circles. If we knew that at a certain event we would see only people we already were acquainted with, we'd be a lot more likely to go… and the event would be pretty much useless in terms of making any useful connections.

Recently a software-developer client invited me to a happy hour to celebrate the hiring of a new executive. I had been pretty minimally involved with them, writing a blog post once a week for maybe six months, some of the posts ghostwritten over the CEO's name. I was uncomfortable about going, because I knew exactly one person at the company, and had met the CEO only once when we first sat down to talk about working together. So in a scenario even more challenging than a typical networking happy hour, I was sure I would be walking into a situation where everyone knew everyone else, except me. Honestly, I didn't think the CEO would even recognize me after that one brief meeting six months earlier. My hope was it would be a large enough group that I could just quietly blend in, but no.

When I arrived, a hostess led me out to the patio where the gathering was taking place, and I discovered a grand total of about eight people standing in a circle. One of them was the CEO, and none of them was the person I actually knew. There would be no hiding.

The CEO looked up and spotted me, and a big smile spread across his face. He waved me over and made a space in the circle. Quietly he said to me, "I'm so glad you came," and then announced to the rest, "This is Jim. He's the guy who makes me sound really smart."

It went pretty well from there. How foolish would I have been to skip that event because I feared the unknown?

We would often see similar situations play out in the context of scouting. Most of the membership of Boy Scout Troop 328 came from the Cub Scouts den at our local elementary school. Boys would age out of Cub Scouts and "bridge over" to Boy Scouts… most of them, anyway. So that was our main pipeline of new members, and they would come in as a group.

But boys did join from other Cub Scout dens, and from other Boy Scout troops as well. It was not uncommon for a parent to bring their young man to visit a meeting as they 'shopped' for a troop that was the right fit. This had the potential to be difficult, because 'our' boys who came via the usual pipeline already knew each other. Newcomers from elsewhere often knew no one else in the room, a tough situation at a socially awkward age. We made a conscious effort to be welcoming, and I was always proud of the way our guys opened their arms to newbies. Still, it had to be difficult for any 11-

or 12-year-old to walk into that room… sort of the way you might feel walking into a networking event: "Will they like me?" "What will I say?" "Will I feel stupid?"

This was exactly the situation when a new scout named Alex joined us one night. Not a soul in the room knew him, but Alex turned the situation on its head.

He brought along a Rubik's Cube. And a Rubik's Snake. And a Rubik's some-other-shape-I-don't-remember-from-geometry-class. The other boys, of course, were intrigued and gathered around to ask if they could have a try. Discussions ensued. Ice was broken. Alex did wind up joining our troop and was instantly one of the guys.

(It turned out that these were not just toys for Alex. A math whiz, he competed nationally in Rubik's competitions, which I did not know was a thing.)

You're probably not going to show up at your next business happy hour with a Rubik's Cube (though I have been to events where robotic coolers circulated about the room on wheels, bringing drinks to guests, while another robot opened beer bottles and poured the contents into cups… those were conversation starters, let me tell you). What can you do, then, to overcome that discomfort?

Make it not about you, that's what. Most of us show up at a networking lunch with a primary objective of, say, getting three solid leads. Flip that around and think, "I want to get to know two new people well enough that I can make a connection for them that will be meaningful to their businesses." You just removed all the pressure—and your own whiff of desperation— from the whole scenario. And in the long run that others-first approach will come back to you in far greater measure than snatching a bunch of business cards and blasting the poor souls with emails.

◆ —————— ◆

I still struggle with being in a new group, as most of us do, but if we can learn to embrace that randomness, we wind up in a much better place. It starts with the space between our ears, though… we have to be open to connecting with all the people who bubble up in our lives every day, and open to allowing them to connect with us whether we think they can do anything for us or not. In the long run, those connections are the foundation that allow us to endure life's unexpected earthquakes.

We're all like rocks tumbling around in some giant polisher, and every time we bump into a new person it changes our shape just a little bit, smoothing a rough edge if we're lucky. When we make it a habit to engage and seek out those connections, we give every day a chance to be the Best Damn Day of Our Life.

Scoutmaster Minute
WHAT ELSE ARE WE MISSING?

You've heard enough Scoutmaster Minutes to know that a favorite theme of mine is making sure we take enough time to appreciate what going on around us...

This really happened a couple of years ago in the winter in a Washington, D.C. Metro station during morning rush hour: A guy came in with a violin case, opened it up, left the case on the ground in front of him for people to put money into and started to play. He played Bach for about 45 minutes that morning.

Now, you can imagine how many people must have passed through that subway station in 45 minutes during rush hour... exactly six of them stopped to listen for a few minutes. A few kids tried to stop, but their parents pulled them along and said they didn't have time. Several other people dropped some money in the case on their way by, but didn't stop. It was probably about a typical morning for a street musician.

Except the guy playing the violin was named Joshua Bell. He's a world-renowned violinist, and two nights before he had sold out a concert hall in Boston at an average price of $100 per ticket. The violin he was playing in that Metro station was worth about 3.5 million dollars.

I know we're busy, and especially in morning rush hour we have places we need to be. But it raises the question: if we don't have time to stop and listen to some of the greatest music ever written, played by a world-class musician on a multi-million dollar instrument, what else are we missing?

The Final Scoutmaster Minute

The final Scoutmaster Minute isn't for the scouts... it's for you. And it's more than a minute, so sue me.

I'll admit to being an old soul, even in comparison to my actual age. I was the youngest of four kids by several years, and both my parents were born just as the Great Depression began. Those lean times colored the way they lived their lives, and the way they raised us. We never took a dollar for granted and I still don't.

The point is that I have a somewhat different worldview, I think, than even others my own age. And in fact I've always carried myself in such a way that people thought I was older. (This is great when you're 19 and you want a beer, but the charm wears off once you enter middle age.)

All that background is intended to offer a little street cred when I say this: I believe that we can't yet fully comprehend the technological changes we've lived through, and their impact on us as human beings.

We are collectively the frog in the pot of water: The heat has been turned up in the form of technology raining down on us, and we don't realize we're about to be boiled.

I don't dismiss at all the marvels of technology: that we can hold a device in one hand that has more processing power than our desktop computers did in the 1990s and also offers turn-by-turn directions, great photos, HD video and, well, nearly any other trick we want it to do… that's nothing short of miraculous. That we use all that handheld magic to send each other smiling piles of poo is nothing short of disturbing.

Maybe you, like me, have trouble discerning whether a given commercial is for a movie or a video game because the graphics have gotten that good, and the disruption of entire industries by the likes of Uber, Netflix and Airbnb has been fascinating to live through.

Just the sheer barrage of information—not only ads, but texts and emails and alerts and the hundred other things your phone nags you about each and every day—is unprecedented.

What cost does all this convenience and connectedness carry? Beyond the funhouse-mirror, highlight-reel view we get of other people's lives on social media, leaving us always trying to measure up, what's becoming of our social skills and our attention spans?

Well before the pandemic, my wife and I went with friends to have dinner at a little Italian restaurant in Baltimore's Federal Hill neighborhood. The place is just a small storefront with maybe 15 tables, and when we arrived early on a Sunday evening, exactly none of them had people at them. We had a lovely dinner, taking our time and chatting, and we were there for perhaps two hours.

Here's what we noticed: In that two-hour span, one other couple came in, had a salad or something quick, and left. All the other tables remained empty… but approximately 25 drivers for DoorDash, Uber Eats, etc. came through to pick up carryout orders. It was like a parade going past our table, and we saw some of the same drivers two and three times.

There's nothing wrong with ordering in, of course, but the contrast was striking. Twenty-five people (or couples) chose not to interact with other humans that evening, and a restaurant that a year before would have been filled with convivial chatter had all the ambience of a library, thanks to the combination of mobile apps for carryout food and (probably) Netflix.

The more connected we *get*, the less connected we *are*.

And this shows not just in the standard "millennials don't know how to have a conversation" complaint, but throughout our daily lives. Venture out onto the road—if you dare—and witness all the drivers who consider you merely an obstacle to be overcome rather than a fellow traveler trying to get somewhere just as they are. ("Driving is a team sport played with strangers," says a friend.)

I believe that our current state of connected disconnectedness—to say nothing of the unending shouting and shaming of our political climate—bears more responsibility than we understand for our ever-increasing rates of depression, addiction and violence

This is not just my opinion. A long-term study of eighth-, tenth- and twelfth-graders showed a decline in psychological well-being beginning in 2012, and a direct correlation between increased screen time and decreased happiness.[17] In short, more time online means less time outdoors or exercising or simply interacting with other humans, and the happiest adolescents are the ones who spend the least time engaged with their electronic devices.

This affects all of us, but I have a special concern for the generation that has never known another way. You and I had some years under our

---

17 Twenge, J. M., Martin, G. N., & Campbell, W. K. (2018). Decreases in psychological well-being among American adolescents after 2012 and links to screen time during the rise of smartphone technology.Emotion, 18(6), 765–780.

belts before the advent of the smartphone, after all. And even we are drawn in by the social media platforms and games that are unabashedly engineered to addict us to their use. So we're often in the room with others, but not really *present*, as we mistake digital connections for connectedness.

And it's not just that we're on our devices, it's what we're consuming. On social media we get the skewed, highlight-reel, everyone's-life-is-better-than-mine perspective, while the news, and especially politics, is relentlessly negative, binary and prone to shouting and name-calling. Where's all the stuff in the middle? In other words, where's real life? Not on your screen.

The old computer programming acronym GIGO seems appropriate: Garbage In, Garbage Out.

What to do?

Here's what's *not* to do. Don't be like me.

Don't wait for a tragedy to challenge you into accepting a new role, into stepping up and taking on a worthy pursuit, into trying to be a better person because others are looking to you for leadership. Don't wait until you're kicked out of the nest at work to decide to be what you really want to be. Don't wait for an amazing person to appear in your life and show you how to connect with strangers. Don't wait for some unspecified thing to happen in order to learn just how much more you're capable of.

Take that first, uncertain step today. It doesn't have to be an all-or-nothing move, just put down your phone and *start*.

Cultivate a habit of gratitude. Engage with the people around you whether you know them or not. Launch a side hustle and see if it grows into a better career. Find an opportunity to sharpen your skills as a leader.

Go volunteer somewhere, get outdoors, start getting back into shape, find someone who's struggling and step in to help, teach someone a new skill, take a deeper interest in those around you, or best of all...

Go take a hike.

AFTERWORD

Throughout this book I've been guessing at the questions you've had as you read (like "So what?"). Here's my last guess: "Jim, your Scoutmaster role ended in 2013. You've been an entrepreneur since 2012. What have you done *lately* to get out of your comfort zone?"

Well, as already noted, I now facilitate a monthly business leadership group. Not exactly a Grand Canyon expedition, but that's something.

A couple of years ago I ended a brief, four-decade hiatus from the stage and have now performed in several community theatre productions. It turns out that as actors go, I'm a pretty good singer.

Oh, and I wrote a book.

◆————◆

Another Sunday morning 12 years later, and once again it's me, the newspaper and a cup of coffee (yes, in a scouting mug) in the sunroom.

There are no shocking, life-changing headlines on this day, just the usual fare. And on the lone business page, a wire-service feature sourced from Inc. magazine and titled, "You may be standing in the way of your success."

It's only a few paragraphs long, and it includes the following nugget:

"One way to ensure your own displeasure and discontentment is to never try anything new... it's when we take risks and try something new that we experience an uplift in our emotions and outlook."[18]

And this:

"End the comparison game... Fueled by social media, which is all about comparison, we tend to look for examples of happiness and contentment, but that ends up creating more anxiety."[19]

I smile and move on to the Sports section.

---

18   The Baltimore Sun, January 19, 2020
19   Ibid.

ACKNOWLEDGMENTS

I've always been an "I can do it myself" kind of guy. To my lovely wife's continuing chagrin, I consider it a personal failure to have to ask an employee where to find something in a store, for just one example.

No project like this, however, happens without a lot of help, starting with the aforementioned lovely wife. For more than three decades Monica's love, encouragement and support have kept me moving forward, and never more than in the protracted process of getting this book done. She also managed not to complain too much on the many occasions when her van smelled like sweaty Boy Scouts following a camping weekend. I am grateful to her—and for her—every single day.

There would have been no story here if we didn't have a Boy Scout. Matt now lives in Nashville and works on Music Row, while his sister Megan returned to Baltimore after college and is a surgical ICU nurse. Thanks for the privilege of learning on the job as your parent and Scoutmaster, guys. We couldn't be more proud.

Very few people saw this manuscript before it went to press. Our former neighbor and emergency backup daughter Kimmee was one who did, and her feedback and shameless cheering-on of the project made it better and kept me going.

I consider myself a reasonably skilled writer, but it turns out that what I'm thinking and what actually appears on the page are not always the same thing. In those spots where my word processor did to words what a food processor does to food, editor Kathleen Cahill put the pieces together again and polished things nicely.

Brigid Kemmerer is an immensely successful author of Young Adult fiction and also a pretty cool human being. From the most tenuous of connections she agreed not only to a phone call, but also to have a look at some of the manuscript and offer some very detailed advice and counsel. I hope I'm that kind to strangers someday.

Mike Tich features prominently in the entrepreneurial stories herein, and there's a reason: for more than eight years now he has been a mentor, an invaluable sounding board and a dear friend, not necessarily in that order. My business would be a mere shadow of what it is were it not for him. And as founder of INSIGHT, Mike is also responsible for bringing together the professional peer group that held me accountable and gently prodded me for more than two years to get this book done. A sincere thank you to Ryan, Bart, Brian, Dom, Ron, Janice, Tony and many others who have passed through as guests.

Imaging waking up one Monday morning to discover that no less a personage than Robert Gates had taken time over his weekend to read a draft of your book and offer words of praise. "Gobsmacked" would be a good description of that moment, and I am forever in his debt.

I hope I've made it clear that the story of Troop 328 would have been far different, and not in a good way, without the leadership of Lee Schmelz, Ethan Young and Mike Hardisky, our three Assistant

Scoutmasters. I am eternally grateful for their leadership, and even more gratified by their continued friendship.

No one should ever have to experience an event as shattering as the Browning tragedy, especially as a teenager or pre-teen. The resilience and spirit of the young men of Troop 328 fill me with awe to this day. The virtual circle they formed to shepherd each other through the aftermath, and the love they showed for each other—though they would probably not use that word—were testaments to themselves and their families. I learned something from every single one of them, and from all who followed in the subsequent years.

In the end, all this is just ink on a page until someone picks it up to read it. Thank you for being that person, and for sharing a few hours of your precious time.

ABOUT THE AUTHOR

 Jim Rafferty is a marketing and communications consultant and Principal of JMRketing, LLC, in Baltimore, Maryland. A former radio announcer and program director, Jim now puts three decades of marketing experience to work in helping businesses communicate more effectively with their audiences. Incurably married and the father of two grown children, Jim spends his spare time singing wherever people will listen and sharing cringe-worthy Dad jokes on social media.

To learn more or to book Jim as a speaker/presenter, visit leaderbyaccident.com.

A free ebook edition is available with the purchase of this book.

To claim your free ebook edition:

1. Visit MorganJamesBOGO.com
2. Sign your name CLEARLY in the space
3. Complete the form and submit a photo of the entire copyright page
4. You or your friend can download the ebook to your preferred device

A **FREE** ebook edition is available for you or a friend with the purchase of this print book.

CLEARLY SIGN YOUR NAME ABOVE

Instructions to claim your free ebook edition:
1. Visit MorganJamesBOGO.com
2. Sign your name CLEARLY in the space above
3. Complete the form and submit a photo of this entire page
4. You or your friend can download the ebook to your preferred device

Print & Digital Together Forever.

Snap a photo

Free ebook

Read anywhere

CPSIA information can be obtained
at www.ICGtesting.com
Printed in the USA
JSHW020733060921
18458JS00011B/84